THE SAAS SALES METHOD

FOR ACCOUNT EXECUTIVES:

How to Win Customers

BY JACCO VAN DER KOOIJ

Copyright ©2018. Published by Winning By Design LLC, a Delaware company

All rights reserved as permitted under the United States Copyright Act of 1976. No part of this book may be reproduced, used or distributed in any form or by any means, or stored in a database or archive, without the expressed written consent of the publisher.

The contents of this book were created in the United States of America.

Edited by Fernando Pizarro and Dan Smith

Revision 5.0

ISBN-13: 978-1986270922

ISBN-10: 1986270920

Winning by Design LLC
San Francisco, California
United States of America
For more information, visit www.winningbydesign.com

More from Winning by Design

The SaaS Sales Method for Account Executives: How to Win Customers is part of Winning by Design's Sales Blueprints series. Other books in the series include:

The SaaS Sales Method: The Science and Process of Sales

Blueprints for a SaaS Sales Organization: How to Design, Build and Scale a Customer-Centric Sales Organization

The SaaS Sales Method Fundamentals: How to Have Customer Conversations

The SaaS Sales Method for Sales Development Representatives: How to Prospect for Customers

The SaaS Sales Method for Customer Success & Account Managers: How to Grow Customers

CONTENTS

WINNING THE RELATIONSHIP — 7

1.	**IDENTIFY**	15
2	**DIAGNOSE**	19
2.1	HOW TO DIAGNOSE YOUR CUSTOMER	19
2.2	HOW TO ESTABLISH THE IMPACT	27
2.3	HOW TO IDENTIFY A CRITICAL EVENT	32
2.4	THE DECISION PROCESS	42
2.5	ORCHESTRATING	50
3.	**PRESCRIBE**	59
3.1	SHARE A CUSTOMER STORY	63
3.2	SHOW/DEMO	68
3.3	PROVOKE/CHALLENGE	79
3.4	HANDLING OBJECTIONS	85
4	**SELECT**	89
4.1	DETERMINE DECISION CRITERIA	89
4.2	PRIORITIZE ON IMPACT	94
4.3	COMPETE	99
4.3	STRATEGY	106

5	**PROPOSE A SOLUTION**	**107**
5.1	QUOTE	112
5.2	IMPACT PROPOSAL	112
5.3	CREATING A BUSINESS CASE	116
6	**PAUSE/GO DARK**	**119**
6.1	SET ALERTS	120
6.2	KEEP EDUCATING (FOMO)	121
7	**TRADE**	**123**
7.1	TRADE	123
7.2	NEGOTIATE	124
7.3	PRICE OBJECTIONS	128
7.4	CRAZY IVAN	130
7.5	ACCELERATED CLOSE	131
8	**COMMIT**	**133**
9	**NOT A FIT**	**137**
9.1	DEBRIEF WITH THE CUSTOMER	137
9.2	CONFIRM THE LOSS	138
SUMMARY		**139**
CONCLUSION		**143**
ABOUT WINNING BY DESIGN		**145**

Winning the Relationship

To help customers in a B2B environment, you will deploy a sales methodology which will dictate your sales process. The ideal sales methodology is not the same for every customer or market. For example: You can't expect to apply a $100,000 consultative sales effort to help a customer buy a $5/month service. On the the other hand, you also can't expect to win a $1MM deal spending $5 in effort! This indicates there are different B2B sales methods. B2B sales is governed by the following methodologies.

- **DIY self service:** A complete end-to-end web experience where customers complete a purchase online.

- **Transactional selling**: Help a customer buy the solution they picked themselves often through online research. These customers often are in a hurry and ready to buy.

- **Solution selling:** Customers already understand their problem and want sales to address specific issues with products and services. Customers buy in days to weeks.

- **Consultative selling**: The customer does not fully understand the problem. Sales has to diagnose the customer's situation to determine the right solution. Sales can take 6-18 months.

- **Provocative selling**:[1] Sales experts can identify customers who will face a problem before they themselves know. They provoke a customer executive into action. Often applied to innovative solution this B2B sales methodology takes anywhere between 3 to 9 months.

---

1   Philip Lay, Todd Hewlin, Geoffrey Moore, "In a Downturn Provoke Your Customers," https://hbr.org/2009/03/in-a-downturn-provoke-your-customers, (March, 2009).

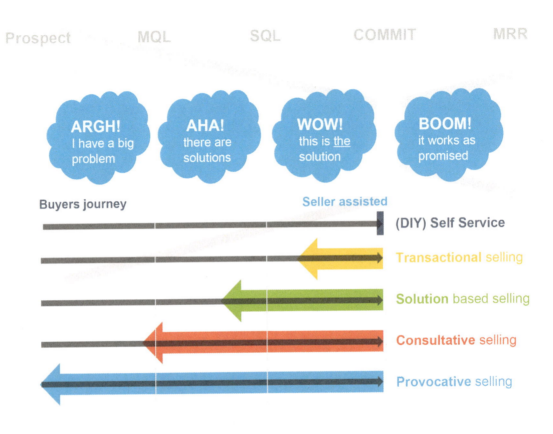

Figure 1: Sales methodologies based on a customer's experience

Transactional selling

The transactional sales process is a reactionary one. Customers know what they want and they are price shopping. They may be willing to forfeit a specific feature if it can save them a lot of money. In transactional sales, customers don't value the role salespeople perform and prefer that salespeople be excluded from the process altogether, or be replaced by web-based and text/chat-based communications in which they get to-the-point, short answers.

Figure 2: Transactional selling in which customers do most of the education on their own

When to use? Transactional selling is best used in high-volume, high-velocity, inbound, low-cost models. Think of selling <$1,000 ACV, <30 day sales cycle, and 20+ deals/month per Account Executive (AE).

Solution selling

The solution sales process is also a reactionary process. A customer understands the problem and has a pretty good idea of what solution they are looking for. They are not quite price shopping (which would make it transactional), and are looking at specific features for which they are willing to pay more. They may have narrowed things down to 2 or 3 providers all by themselves by the time they reach out to you.

Figure 3: Solution selling, often following an inbound lead

When to use? Solution selling is best used in medium-volume, high-velocity-based inbound models. Think of selling $5,000 ACV, ~30 day sales cycle, and cutting 5-10 deals/month per AE.

Consultative selling

In consultative selling, you are investing early-on in the customer to educate them on what is important based on what you have seen in the market. You are educating the customer and help them understand the real problem and how to look for the right solution. Your experience is represented in their requirements in the form of features and functionality. You may help them write the RFP/RFQ. This kind of deal is often marked by a Proof Of Concept, which makes the consultative sale significantly longer. During the consultative sales process, we gradually ramp up the quality of resources used as we navigate through the customer's organization.

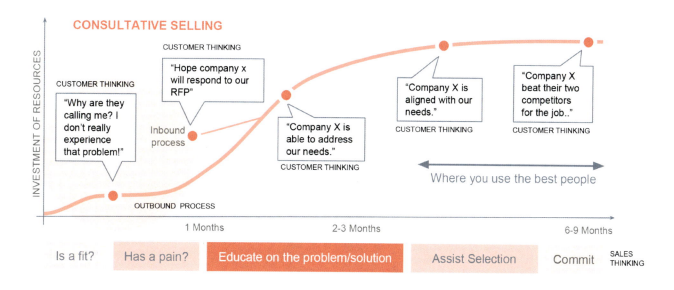

Figure 4: Consultative selling often following outbound lead generation/development

When to use? Consultative selling is best used when you are selling platform-like solutions involving a number of decision makers. Think of a CRM for $20-100k ACV, 6-18 month sales cycle, and 1-3 deals/quarter per AE.

Provocative selling

When you are representing an innovative solution that challenges the status quo you cannot rely on the consultative process, as most customers do not realize there is a problem lurking. In particular, an RFP/RFQ which is a process designed to flush out lowest price/minimal spec. Thus you have to rely on provocative selling, which has gained popularity through a methodology called the Challenger sale.

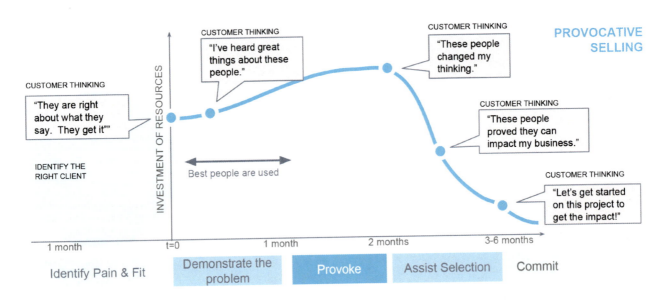

Figure 5: Provocative selling only recommended for deployment on specific accounts

When to use? Provocative selling is best used when selling innovative solutions that address a CEO's top issue. Think of a revolutionary way to do ERP, 6-9 month sales cycle, $250k ACV and 1-2 deals/quarter per AE.

Simplified sales process

All of these sales approaches use the same activities, differentiated in four key processes:

- **Educating**: Helping the market understand the problem, the impact and potential solutions.
- **Prospecting**: Reach out to customers who have pain and are a fit, and setting up a discovery call.
- **Winning**: Diagnose whether a customer can be helped and assist them through a buying experience.
- **Growing**: Help the customer to onboard and use the service to realize the impact.

Below is the winning process, which consists of nine main activities (blue) and sits between the prospecting process (red) and the onboarding process (green).

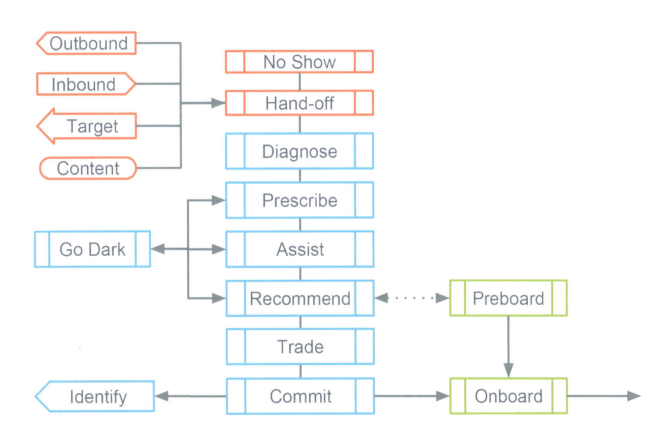

Figure 6: WBD's simplified customer-centric winning process

Table 1 Applying the sales activities across the different sales approaches

Section	Users	SMB	Mid Market	Enterprise
Methodology	**Transactional**	**Solution**	**Consultative**	**Provocative**
Prospecting	Inbound	Outbound / Content	Target	Identify
Diagnose		Impact /Critical Event	Decision Process	Orchestrate
Prescribe	Trial	Demo	Proof of Concept	Workshop
Assist		Decision Criteria	Compete	Provoke
Recommend		Customer Quote	Impact Proposal	Business Case
Trade	Buy Online	Trade	Objections	Negotiate
Commit		P/O	MSA	+ SoW
Go Dark	Nurture	Outbound	Alerts	Provoke

1. Identify

In the Prospecting book, we learned there are four processes in identifying a prospective customer; customers who have experienced a pain and approach us via an *inbound* request, a group of customers we *outbound* to because the are a fit and are likely to experience pain we can solve, *targeting* several people at a small group of customers, and educating the market through *content*. From an Account Executive's perspective, we now are *adding a 5th prospecting process; Identify*.

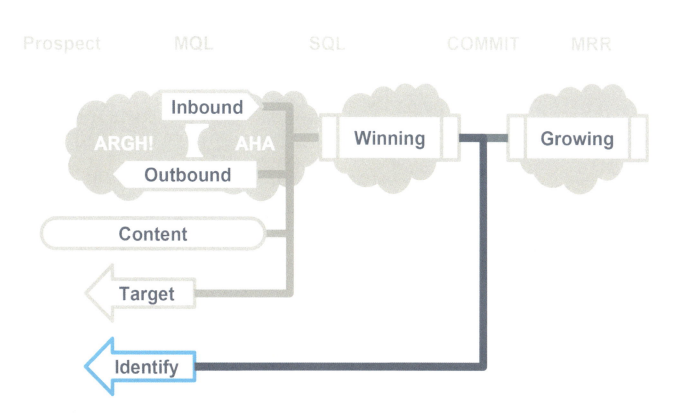

Figure 7: Where identifying fits

Identify is the process that is performed by an AE and starts *following* a COMMIT. We use this process to immediately identify any other sizable potential customer that has the same circumstances. For example: A brand-new committed customer sells a security service and has characteristics similar to the committed customer, as outlined in the figure below.

Figure 8: Different ways of finding relevance to identify prospective customers

Based on this, we can now identify a new account based on a strong entry point that has relevance to this win, for example:

- Other financial institutions (market segmentation).
- Companies located in the area geographically similar to the account (regional segmentation).
- Companies that face the same security issue across different segments (product segmentation).
- Other companies that are looking to achieve the same impact (impact segmentation).
- Other CIOs that know the CIO we worked with at the bank (personal network).

The most common one is product segmentation (they are a fit for our product), but this is also the hardest to secure as they rarely have a pain.

TARGETING EXERCISE Use of relevance to identify a list or prospective customers

When preparing your questions, work backwards from the value proposition that you expect to have the biggest impact, based on your persona.

Table 6.2 Identify a prospective customer based on relevance

Relevance	Identified Accounts
	Other companies in the same market segment
	Other companies in the customer's vicinity
	Other companies having the same problem

Relevance	Identified Accounts
	Other companies looking for the same impact
	....
	....
	Other people with the same problem known personally by the buyer
	....
	....
	....

2 Diagnose

> The ABC of Customer-Centric Sales: **Always Be Curious.**
>
> *Jacco van der Kooij*

When you are talking to a customer, you must not communicate that you are "selling" before you understand their diagnosis. Many sales professionals feel that they have to show the customer their product, pitch some insights, and hope the customer will see how it can solve their problem.

This is prescribing a solution before diagnosing, and in most jobs is considered illegal. Great sales professionals start by asking questions to diagnose the situation, without emphasizing the company they work for or service they sell. They engage not with the intent to sell, but with the intent to understand the customer's situation.

2.1 How to Diagnose Your Customer

There are three different kinds of questions. Sequencing these questions allows you to properly diagnose a customer's problems. Establishing their situation, the pain they encounter, and the impact of solving those pains all lead to the value proposition of their needed solution.

The principle of this technique requires you to increase engagement through a series of questions.

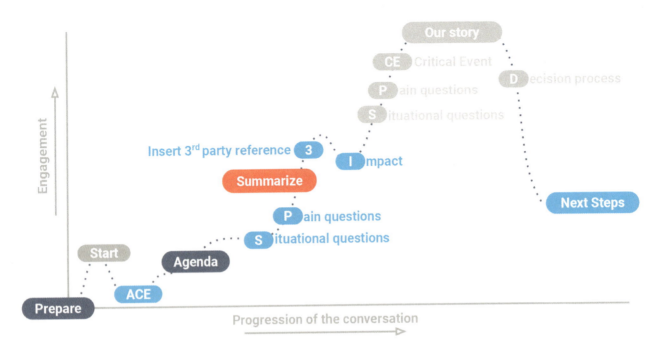

Figure 9: Diagnose by mastering sequencing of questions in the spiced framework

STEP 1 Prepare for the meeting

Goal: Don't get rushed into the call, take your time, be ready.

Send out courtesy email with the details, set up your browser tabs, make sure the technology works! Perform your last-minute research, and be on the call 1-2 minutes before the call starts.

STEP 2 Open the conversation

Goal: Set yourself up as a friendly professional.

Inquire about what is going on in their world – but do not focus on cliche rapport building like weather, sports, or nearby coffee shops. Speak about relevant industry news. Ask who will be joining the call. This is also a good time to mention (ask for approval) that you will be recording the call. What you should NOT do is start political or sports debates, or worse, how great the weather is in California. Keep it short!

STEP 3 ACE the start of the meeting

Goal: Structure the meeting, establish "why we are speaking and what we will accomplish."

Appreciate you joining the call. We have you on the schedule until 11:30 today, does that still work for you?

I have a hard stop 5 minutes early.

I will make sure we end in time for you. Typically this call ends with us deciding this could be a good fit for us to move forward – but if you realize what we discuss won't meet your requirements, will you interrupt and let me know?

Sounds great!

STEP 4 Set the agenda of the call

Goal: Establish what they would like to discuss today after you've set the stage.

Confirm the agenda by asking each person on the call what they are looking to get out of today's meeting. Make sure you write it down, and make sure that you address each and everyone on the call.

Our agenda today is (XYZ). May I ask, what do you want to make sure we cover on this call?

I also want to learn about how the product works and get an idea if it can help me solve XYZ problem.

Okay. So you want to learn about how to address your problem and how our product works. Anything else?

Yes and get an idea on your price.

Yes we can tackle that too. Mike did you want to add anything?

I'd love to learn more about your global support.

Support, got it!

Use what you learn by asking a question about what they'd like to get out of the call to structure what comes next.

Goal: Establish their priorities

That's a lot to talk about in the allotted time. May I ask what is the most pressing issue?

How the product works and how it can help me solve XYZ problem.

Okay – why don't we start with those two topics and address the others at the end?

Sounds like a plan.

STEP 5 Diagnose their situation and desired outcome

Goal: Diagnosis of the situation using the S and P questions. In later parts of the conversation, use I questions to go deeper and elaborate.

How many employees do you have that submit expense reports every week?

We have 12 people.

Which tools do they use today?

They use Excel spreadsheets.

Do you have challenges with timely filing of reports?

The team often files them with finance on the last day of the month – our busiest time!

How does that impact your business?

The finance team works overtime, causing lots of __frustration__.

STEP 6 Summarize the conversation

Goal: Establish that you heard your customer, and understand the situation and the pain(s) it is causing.

*So let me know if I've got this right: You have 12 people on the team that file expense reports on the last day of the month, using Excel spreadsheets, which your team has to manually process during the busiest time of the month, resulting in the team working overtime and getting **frustrated**. Did I get that right?*

Yup, you got it.

PRO TIP Did you see how you mirrored the emotional word frustration? This develops a mutual trust with your customers as you demonstrate that you are listening closely to them. More on this active listening strategy below.

- JACCO VAN DER KOOIJ

STEP 7 **Provide a 3rd-party reference**

Goal: Show empathy, provide a use-case, establish yourself as an expert.

That definitely sounds like a challenging situation. You're not alone in feeling frustrated: Michelle from Acme, who is also a VP of Operations like you, felt the same way. She found that digitizing her workflow and automating several tasks reduced her cost on overtime and employee dissatisfaction.

Does that resonate with you?

Of course! How did she solve it?

This was an executive priority for her company, and was able to complete the project in 3 weeks.

That's exactly what we're looking to do.

STEP 8 Identify value by presenting the Impact of how your solution could help

Goal: Begin to transition from emotional to rational decision-making and quantify the value of your solution.

In this case, we can conclude that the situation happens 12x a year, learn how many employees work overtime, estimate the amount paid for overtime per employee, and then estimate the annual dollars spent on working on overtime and compare that against your solution.

In order to help you get the best solution, I'd like to clarify. Since this sounds like something that happens every month, 12x a year, how many employees have to work overtime and for how many hours each?

There are 4 employees that work 20 hours each.

So with accountants making about $120k/year, which breaks down to 10k/mo, and there is about 80 hours of overtime per month total – this is costing you $60k per year and ruining employee morale. Does that sound about right?

Yes – that sounds about right.

Let's get you something better. Based on what you've described, it sounds like our solution can definitely help. And good news, it will pay for itself in 6 weeks. Since you mentioned end of the month is your busiest time, how about we get started first week of next month?

SPI EXERCISE Work backwards to build your diagnosis questions and share 3rd-party insight

When preparing your questions, work backwards from the value proposition that you expect to have the biggest impact, based on your persona.

Breakdown	Your Answers
Who is the Persona? What is their title?	Persona: Job title:
What is their biggest value proposition or value driver to your solution?	Value proposition: Impact it has on the business:
Who is a customer you know of who benefited greatly from this in the past	3rd-party reference:
What is an Impact question that you could ask that would lead to the value proposition answer above?	I:
What are some pain or problems that result if their main value proposition is not solved?	P1: P2:
What is their situation that would help create this pain? (Use Excel, have 5 offices globally etc.)	S1: S2: S3:

STEP 8 Next Steps

The key to the Recap is to link it to the **ACE** at the beginning of the call.

- **SUMMARIZE** what you went over today
- **ASK** if their questions were addressed
- **RECAP** the agreed action
- **ASK** if they are ready to move forward
- Agree to the **NEXT STEP**
- Agree to a **DATE**
- Discuss **WHO** should be present

2.2 How to Establish the Impact

SaaS has become extremely competitive, as almost every service sits on the same cloud infrastructure, uses a very similar color scheme (e.g., blue for social, green for predictive), so competing can quickly become feature-to-feature combat. This is not to the benefit of the customer, as they are often bamboozled into paying for features they're never going to need. As a sales professional, you can play a key role in helping to avoid this early on by identifying the impact.

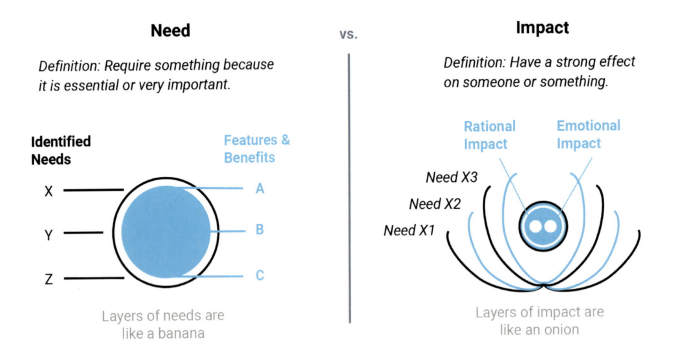

Figure 10: Visualize impact vs. need

Understand the impact journey

In the picture above, you will notice on the left a traditional focus on the customer's identified needs, translating those into features and benefits. On the right, you see that the customer's need is actually more like an onion with endless layers that, through the art of asking questions, has to be peeled – to the core. Often 6-7 layers deep (6-7 questions deep!), you can find the underlying impact of the need.

This impact determines the difference between nice-to-have vs. must-have, and understanding this concept is what separates a good AE from a great AE.

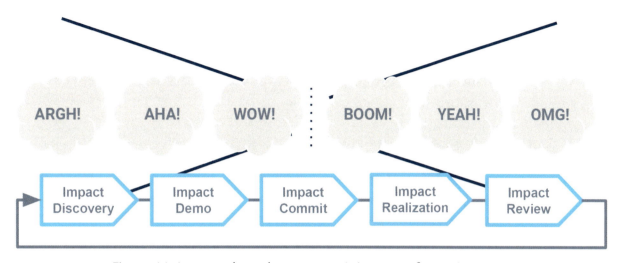

Figure 11: Impact along the customer's journey of experiences

This impact is best identified by talking to a customer. As an AE you have to come up with a list of meaningful questions to ask on the impact of the service (see Diagnose)

How do we measure impact?

Today there are three kinds of software value propositions that impact a business. You need to know which type of impact is most important to your customer.

Impact 1:	Impact 2:	Impact 3:
Reduce COST	**Improves EXPERIENCE**	**Increase REVENUE**
By using the service, you are reducing costs by X% annually, or by $2,000/month.	The 24/7 support teams keep you on the air. It takes only 2 clicks to get to... vs. 8 clicks... these charts identify the action.	With this service you grow your revenue by xx%, or by $2,000/account per month.

Table 3: Three kinds of impact

Of these three, selling software that increases revenue is the easiest to sell, since growth is still the most important priority.

Increase Revenue: The need to grow overrules cost-reduction because growth increases the value of the overall business, as it brings in more logos, users, and best practices. Thus it is not a surprise that products that grow revenue enjoy shorter sales cycles and can be sold at a higher price. Think of products such as Lead Generation and Sales Acceleration software.

Reduce Cost: A solution that increases revenue hinges on an effectiveness-driven model. Compare this to a solution that reduces cost, which hinges on an efficiency-driven value proposition. Buying a solution that reduces cost is the easiest, however it operates at a lower price or rather a lower profit, and this makes the business dependent on volume of deals. Think of companies selling online storage.

In both cases, the solution is sold at about 10% of the impact created.

Customer Experience: Improving the customer experience and/or interaction results in productivity improvement and it often looks and feels like cost-reduction software; better-to-understand dashboards, easier to operate, improved collaboration, reduced risk, find better candidates. These value propositions are one step removed from revenue increases or cost reductions. Collaboration products, productivity tools, business intelligence software, human resources information systems, and security products all fit into this category.

Each of these approaches can lead to a healthy business. The key part is understanding the type of value proposition your start-up offers and matching the GTM and customer success strategy to it.

IMPORTANT: When selling an effectiveness/efficiency solution, it has to provide its rationale impact of revenue increase/cost reduction month-over-month, year-over-year. Sooner or later, the impact no longer warrants the investment. Customer Experience solutions provide a far longer runway for success. Think of a CRM solution.

The psychology of impact

The roots of why Customer Experience has a longer runway lies in understanding that there are two ways impact is perceived, each of which relates to how humans make decisions. Rational, which is measurable using facts and figures, and emotional, which is about feelings and experiences. The research shows that people tend to make an emotional decision, then validate with facts and figures.[2] Thus emotional impact supersedes the rational impact.

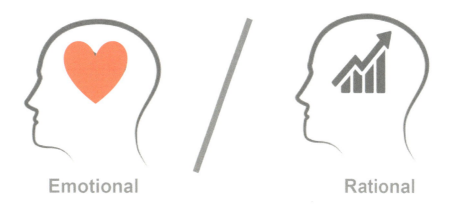

Figure 12: Emotional impact supersedes rational impact

GREAT EXAMPLE **Emotional impact over rational impact**

In the example that follows, you find that the customer's "feeling about missing out" supersedes that of "22% growth." This is critical to understand, as it may be hard for your company to promise 22% growth, but you may be very able to open up the Chinese market. Focus on solving the right problem.

---

2. R. Levine, "The Power of Persuasion: How We're Bought and Sold" (2003)

Frances, in your 10K statement you indicate you plan to expand internationally and in particular to China. Did I get that right??

That is right. We need to grow by 22% and that can only come from China.

Have you looked at other regions?

Yes, but we are feeling we are missing out on China. We are not doing it right.

What makes you feel like you are missing out?

Our competition is reporting huge growth in China...

2.3 How to Identify a Critical Event

A critical event is an event that is so important that it drives the decision. Think of an event such as the launch of a product, a particular date such as "Black Friday," or a circumstance such as hitting 1,000,000 users. The chart on the next page identifies 3 product launches for example.

In the chart, you notice that over time the priority increases from nice-to-have, to need-to-have, and at one point even reaches must-have. It is critical to determine where you are in this picture. As the priority drops, a customer may go dark, leading you to believe that the "budget is spent," not realizing the conditions may change in your favor in which the priority will increase again. Even better... understanding their situation, you may outline the full impact of your service and how it can solve other challenges the customer may experience, which will help you increase the priority!

Compelling event vs. critical event

We must distinguish between a compelling event and a critical event: A critical event is an event that carries consequences if the deadline is not met. A compelling event is something that is more of a nice-to-have that indicates interest, but not explicit action to solve within a specific timeframe.

Compelling Event	Critical Event
What time do you need this by?	*What time do you need this by?*
I need X done by Y date.	*I need X done by Y date.*
What happens if you miss that date?	*What happens if you miss that date?*
It probably moves to next month.	*I am going to get fired!*

It may be hard for you to establish what a critical event is; you should always have a list of top 5-10 common critical events that you run into.

Critical event date

The key is to – early on – establish what the critical event is. The key question to ask is: "When do you need this service to be live by?" THEN followed by "…and what happens if you miss that date?" This simple question will let you know if the event is "compelling" or "critical." As the customer shares the critical event, you can now say: "In case you have to have this live by {{date}} to get this {{impact}} or otherwise you {{consequence}} … how can we help you avoid that?" You can now work your way back from the date and start peeling the onion.

IMPORTANT: Note that sometimes you may identify a critical event, but due to local culture/events/holidays, the deadline is still flexible.

Critical event timeline[3]

A critical event is like the end result of a delicious recipe when cooking a meal. In order to achieve your desired outcome, the recipe tells you what to do in what order. And following the identification of a critical event, you must uncover all the steps that need to happen.

---

3   To learn more about this we recommend you read Daniel J. Adams award-winning book on BUILDING TRUST, GROWING SALES on his web site: www.trusttriangleselling.com

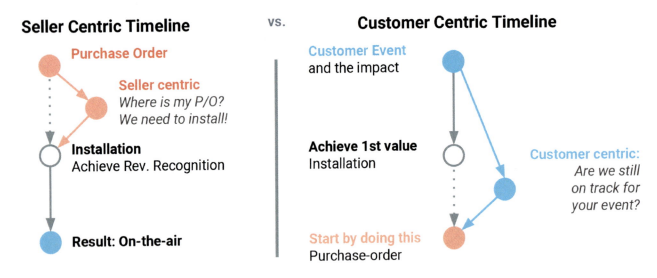

Figure 13: Visualization of a critical event timeline

Instead of determining when you need the P/O from the customer, you need to start with the customer needs in mind. When does the customer need the desired impact? Then work your way back. For example, if the customer has a sales kick-off on July 7, they need your new sales acceleration solution for their team in place by end of June.

This means they need to have your quote submitted to legal by June 15 for execution on June 22. If you do not receive the P/O on the June 22nd, you don't call them up and say: "Jennifer where is my P/O?"… but instead you ask "Jennifer are we still on track for the launch of your service on July 7th." The critical event is not getting a P/O – it is the customer going live.

 IMPORTANT: Once a critical event timeline has been created together with the customer, you need to confirm this in an email. This has to be a new email thread. This allows you later on to help your coach etc.

Critical event timeline in the confirmation email

A critical event timeline is a short standalone email that solely talks about the critical event. This cannot be part of a two-page email with all kinds of actions. Below an example.

`GREAT EXAMPLE` **Critical event follow-up email and how to use it**

Subject: SKO July 15 / PO May 29 / Decision May 8

Dear Mary,

Thank you for taking the time today to talk. To have us hit your July 15 Sales Kick-Off, we need to get the proposal memorialized in an order by May 29th. Based on your purchasing process, I put the following timeline together to hit that date:

July 15 – Your Sales Kick-off

July 2 – Integration and Staff Training

June 1 – Request for Web Developer

May 29 – Process Purchase Order to hit monthly cycle

May 15 – Legal Review of SLA Agreement

May 8 – The project team concludes <our company> offers the right solution

Did I capture this correctly?

With kind regards,

Mark

This is an important email as it help you reduce the chances of "going dark," but also, if other stakeholders are involved during the project, you can forward this to keep all the noses in the same direction. A common use is when the customer's Legal (outside) counsel gets involved and says they need 2 weeks instead of 1.

Rather than you a) agreeing or b) creating tension between you and the legal team which may carry consequences in your negotiations, you can now forward the email to both legal counsel and Mary and ask Mary to deal with this.

Subject: FW: SKO July 15 / PO May 29 / Decision May 8

Mary – Please find cc'd Scott in Legal he indicated that realistically 2 weeks are needed. Can you help coordinate and advise if/how you would like to adjust the timeline of the project?

Best – Mark

EXERCISE Uncover the critical event of a customer

As a sales professional, you need to absolutely be aware of any potential critical events for your customer. Some happen annually, such as sales kickoffs, end of fiscal years, and holidays. Others can be business-dependent, such as "Dreamforce," or "Product X Launch." Use a real customer call you have had in the last 2 weeks.

Key Information	Your Notes
What was their critical event? (E.g. Sales Kickoff upcoming and want to announce a new tool to get reps excited)	
What was the critical event date	
What was the consequence if they missed that date?	
What was the critical event timeline: What needed to happen (in order) to hit that date? (in reverse chronological order)	
What are the critical event dates of your business	

Identifying a critical event with an educated buyer

In the picture below, you will notice four key moments. Although many would say that #2 is the ideal moment to help a customer, it actually is #4, since the customer has experienced the pain before (in 3). This, in comparison to #1 and #2 where the customer has not yet experienced the pain. This makes the buyer in #4 an educated buyer.

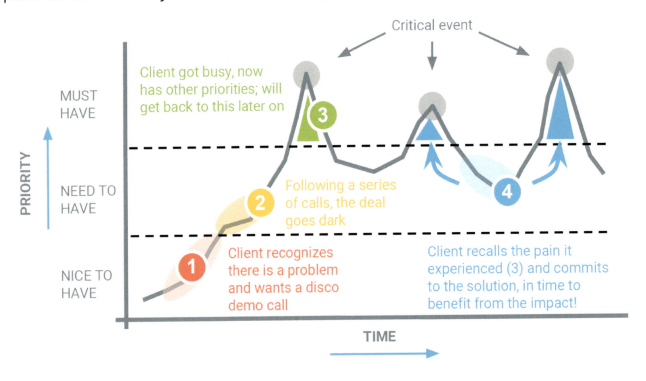

Figure 14: Identifying the level of "pain" a customer is familiar with

Understanding this you should always ask if a customer experienced the pain before. Find out:

- Were you involved in buying the previous solution?
- What was your involvement during the previous purchase?
- How did that process work? Is that still the same process?

GREAT EXAMPLE Critical event timeline

Key Information	Example Critical Event
What is their critical event?	Sales Kickoff is coming up and want to announce a new tool to get reps excited.
What is the critical event date	July 15
Consequence: What happens if you miss the launch of this tool by the sales meeting?	*Weak (rational):* No $$$ benefit *Strong (emotional):* Sales has no new tools to work with. *Very Strong (emotional):* I look bad in front of my team.
What needs to happen to hit that date?	• Need the team trained <takes 1 week>
• What comes before this:	• Tools needs to be integrated <takes 1 hour>
• What comes before this:	• Web Developer available <takes 1 month>
• What comes before this:	• Processes order <takes about 1 week>
• What comes before this:	• Legal agrees to terms <takes about 2 weeks>
• What comes before this:	• Quote/Proposal tuned <takes about 1 week>

THE SAAS SALES METHOD FOR ACCOUNT EXECUTIVES

Relationship between critical event and impact

As depicted below, there is a direct relationship between Impact and Critical Event. They go together like pepper and salt.

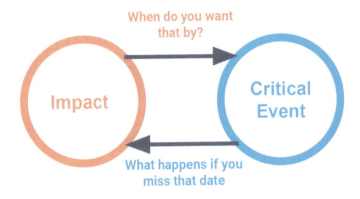

Figure 15: There is a direct relationship between critical event and impact

 **PRO TIP** If you can impact a customer's business, they will make it a priority and create a budget for it, unless there is a specific reason that they cannot take on this project right now. Perhaps they are currently retooling a part of their IT infrastructure or a key stakeholder is out on leave. Therefore, it may help to ask the customer if there is any reason why they could NOT implement a solution in the next ninety days.

- Dominique Levin

EXERCISE Identify critical events based on past customers

Customer Name	Their Critical Event	Questions To Uncover
Example: Acme	*Example:* Dreamforce – Biggest Trade Show in their Industry	*Example:* Are you attending Dreamforce (booth)? How many leads do you get from… How do you follow-up to those leads… Do I understand that, due to this influx of leads, you don't differentiate between important and unimportant leads?

2.4 The Decision Process

Historically, most B2B deals used a hierarchy model, in which getting to the most senior decision maker resulted in the best results. Today we find that more and more decisions are made by committee, or consensus, and that senior involvement, although still important, no longer yields the best results.

This comes from the radical change in pricing models. Conventional B2B deals were often measured in hundreds of thousands of dollars, and the only ones with such an approval authority were the VP/CxO's of the company. However, today we see most B2B sales using a subscription driven model (Software as a Service, or SaaS) resulting in fraction of the original spend. This lower spend gives a low-level manager the purchasing power on something that can impact the entire organization for years to come.

This has resulted in a new process where decisions are made by consensus by a committee. Consensus decisions are not new; historically they were known as buying centers and commonly used to navigate across a complex decision process (such as a government) with multi millions of dollars at stake.

What is new is that we see buyers behavior trending away from the hierarchical decision process toward a consensus-driven decision process for organizational, and cultural reasons.

Hierarchy vs. consensus decision process

In the picture that follows, you see on the left a traditional "decision tree." Users roll up into managers, who in turn roll up toward an executive who gathers the info and makes the decision. In the hierarchy model, it is common for the Executive to overrule the decision based on the merits of a more future-proof solution, for example, only to find that users hate the chosen solution and refuse to use it.

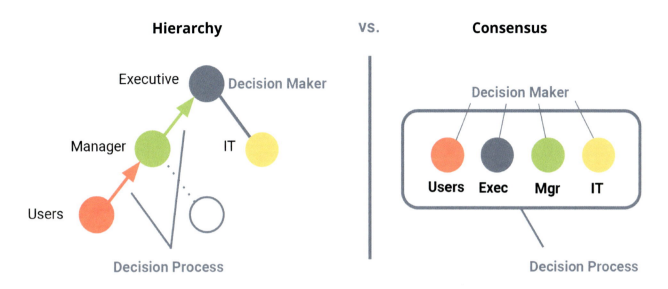

Figure 16: Hierarchical vs. committee decision process

On the right, you see that the hierarchy of the decision tree has collapsed into that of a committee where everyone has become "the decision maker." In the case of a committee, the executive no longer plays the key role, but rather the end-user who has to work with the chosen solution every day. The user will be guided in the decision process by the UI/UX criteria, the manager may favor dashboards and reporting, whereas the executive's primary concerns is to achieve the impact and to make sure a proper decision process was followed. The committee must reach a consensus to act.

This indicates that one of the first priorities is to determine what kind of decision process is being followed. Next an example question followed by a brief description on both processes.

Key question to ask...

Have you bought a solution like this before?

Followed by…

What was the decision process?

IMPORTANT: It is the responsibility of the AE to identify the decision process even if the sponsor is unwilling to provide insights into this.

Understanding the hierarchy decision process

In the hierarchy model of the past decade, we perceive the most important roles to be the VP or CxO level. Why? Because it was based on purchasing authority against seniority aligned along brackets of PO size (e.g. Manager $10K, VP $100K, and CxO over $500K). The price of B2B software was measured in hundreds of thousands if not millions of dollars. This required CxO level approval.

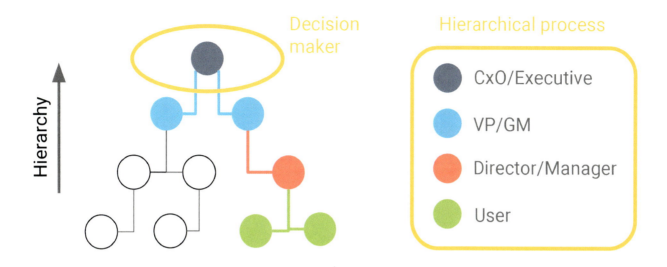

Figure 17: Hierarchy model often with a single decision maker

In organizational selling, you identify all the people involved in the decision, and structure them hierarchically you then maneuver over time to the most senior level associated based on the price of your product. This model follows the following steps:

STEP 1 Establish who is involved – often based on the value of the product you are selling.

STEP 2 Identify the hierarchy – who reports into who – often based on title (LI Sales Navigator).

STEP 3 Establish value proposition per role/title.

STEP 4 Sell into the highest level you can achieve to gain support.

STEP 5 Move up a level repeat STEP 3 and 4 until you get to the decision maker.

It is the job of the AE to align the company's resources to the point that executives line up. This means that as an AE, you need to achieve coverage to at least the Director level, and if possible at a VP level. The higher you go, the better. This way you can level your VP with their VP to discuss the outlines of the deal. Your VP in turn will bring in your CEO to meet with their CEO to discuss the partnership... and so on.

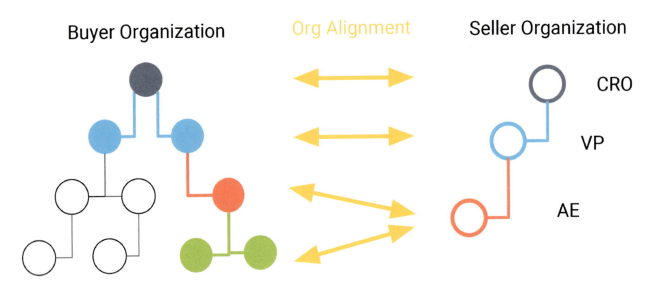

Figure 18: Aligning seniority between buyer and seller organizations (3x3 matrix)

If you bring in your VP to a manager meeting, it is often frowned upon for the VP to then go over the head of the manager and talk to the VP. So make sure that you're staying aware of the reporting structure and that you are aware when you are about to step on someone's toes.

In hierarchical selling, navigating to a senior level is the single most important skill an AE can have. This is reflected by organizations who hire AEs and "pay" for their AE to have access to the CxO based on previous experience selling to this person.

IMPORTANT: It is the responsibility of the AE to navigate to senior levels even if the sponsor is unwilling to provide support. A customer may block you in favor of a fiefdom (def: An organization or department over which one dominant person or group exercises control). In the hierarchical model, you must reach the decision maker.

Keys for sales teams with this approach

- The Sales Development Rep (SDR) identifies the organizational structure using LinkedIn.
- The AE creates a 3x3 model in which 3 people of the seller are aligned with 3 people of the buyer.
- The AE gets as high as possible then involves execs to expand reach at more senior levels.

EXAMPLE **Executive introduction**

If you find yourself in a position to introduce your VP or CEO, you need to be be comfortable introducing that person with a short note. The common mistake is for your to write a detailed report. Below is an outline of how you can create a short and to-the-point introduction with the right level of detail.

{{CEO Name}},

For the past few weeks, we have been working with {{person x}}, {{person y}} and {{person z}} on your team to meet your goal of _____. At this time I'd like to introduce you to _____, my VP (cc'd). She expressed interest in sharing some valuable insights with you about how other customers were able to achieve similar goals.

With kind regards,

{{Your name}}

PS: Below a brief summary of what has been accomplished to date.

The consensus model

The consensus model brings together all those involved in the process of buying, installing, using, and maintaining. Such a committee looks well beyond financial drivers, and it is tasked to address questions such as:

1. Will the Users actually use it?
2. Does it make the lives of the users better?
3. Does it work within our infrastructure (across the entire company).
4. Does the manager use and gain benefit from the reports?
5. Does the dashboard help make better decisions?
6. Is this the most effective and efficient use of our money?
7. ... at this time?

Questions like this must be addressed, but over time. For example, there is no reason to talk about the financial impact if the users are already railroading it. This creates a chronological approach where A needs to happen before B before C. An example can be found on the next page.

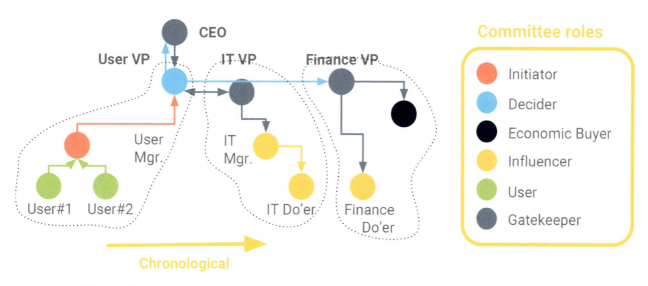

Figure 19: Decision makers spread across the company organized by buying roles

Eventually the last voice on the committee is that of the economic buyer who is held accountable for achieving the "impact" against the investment in both money and time. Note that in a committee model, the most valuable role is NOT the most senior decision maker, nor the economic buyer. Literally anyone in the committee can derail the decision at any time. To start off, we need to identify the person who initiated the deal and learn what impact they wish to achieve. As you can see in the picture above, User1 kick-started the relationship. Often these kind of users can be found, as their LinkedIn profile reflects their innovative accomplishments "first to implement ___" or "Level 3 certified in ____" .

 **IMPORTANT:** In the consensus model, it is the job of the AE to identify all stakeholders / across departments – even if the buyer is not capable. Many sponsors may not have the depth to understand that IT, Legal, and Support need to be involved. Do not blindly trust that your "buyer" knows the buying process. This maybe the first time they are buying this kind of solution, whereas you are an expert.

THE SaaS SALES METHOD FOR ACCOUNT EXECUTIVES – 49

2.5 Orchestrating

In committee models and in provocative sales, it is key to "orchestrate" the communication. What needs to happen first, what next, who needs to be involved when and where. You may want to start at the CEO level with a 50-person company, but if you are trying to sell to Amazon – cold-calling Jeff Bezos without company-specific context can and will adversely impact the deal.

EXAMPLE **Orchestrating a deal over time**

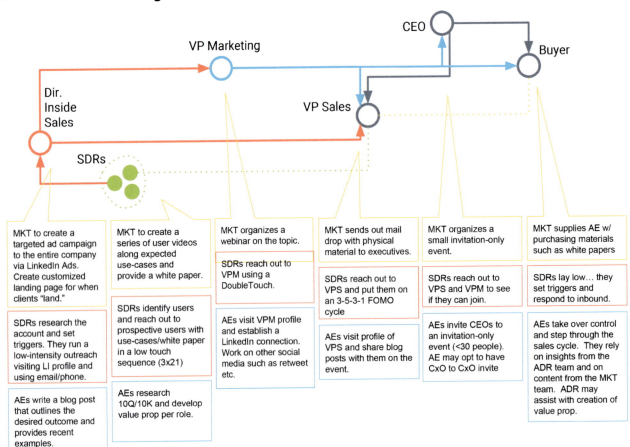

Figure 20: Orchestrated plan

50 – THE SAAS SALES METHOD FOR ACCOUNT EXECUTIVES

1. Enthusiastic user #1 runs into a problem, finds a solution.

2. He runs it by a friend, user #2 who loves it too.

3. They get the User Manager to participate in the trial.

4. User Manager sees the benefits from the reports and runs it up to the VP.

5. The VP sees the financial benefits and is happy to hear his team is excited about it, so he does not have to worry about "retaining" them.

6. VP runs a snapshot value prop by the CEO with the impact it has on the business.

7. The CEO says to make sure that IT is OK with it, and that Finance has it in the budget.

8. User VP asks IT VP to check it.

9. IT VP delegates it to the IT Manager/Do'er. Do'er runs the analysis to make sure it runs on the stack and it conforms to security rules.

10. Do'er gives the thumbs up to the Manager, who gives the thumbs up to the IT VP.

11. IT VP lets User VP know.

12. The User VP asks the Finance VP to get budget.

13. Finance VP delegates to the Finance Do'er.

14. Finance Do'er runs the numbers and says it fits.

15. Finance VP lets User VP know.

16. User VP tasks a Buyer to "buy."

17. Buyer asks Manager to perform a trial and obtain pricing from three vendors.

Mapping relationships

Both for Consensus and Hierarchy decisions, it is important to understand the sentiment of the buyer.

Icon	Sentiment	Description
♥	Loves Us	Strong emotional for us due to great interaction.
+	Positive	Positive interaction and leaning towards us in the decision.
=	Neutral	Has insight and has appeared neutral in their decision.
?	Unknown	Unknown. Do not have insight. Undetermined in their decision.
-	Negative	Has insights and is leaning towards another solution.
👻	Hates us	Strong emotional against us based on bad interaction.

Based on this sentiment, we can now map this to the decision maker process (consensus) in the previous paragraph and we get the following picture.

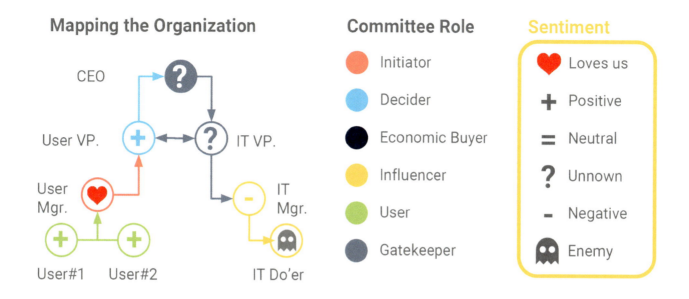

Figure 21: Mapping sentiment of the impending decision to a consensus process

If figure above was a hierarchy process, you might be able to convince the User VP to go to the CEO and gain approval. However in the Consensus model, you are likely going to be derailed by the IT department which, because of the IT Do'er, is not going to support the decision. The IT Do'er may be a proponent of your competitor, having worked with them previously. The action plan is clear: Secure the IT manager and IT VP by setting up meetings with them – and this is important, BEFORE the decision reaches the CEO.

EXERCISE Perform an account readout

STEP 1 Identify a accounts based on I/CE using a recent win.

Account	Similar Win	Impact	Critical Event

STEP 2 Establish the Org Chart

Name	Role

STEP 3 **Identify Impact and Critical Event per key role (at least 3 but no more than 5)**

Critical Event	Impact #1	Impact #2

STEP 4 **Understand the Decision Process. How will the decision "flow" through the organization**

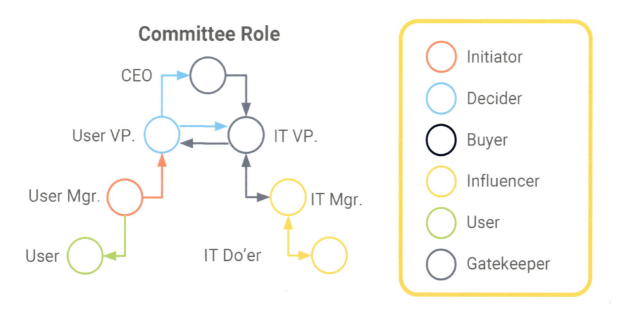

STEP 5 Establish sentiment, identify the areas to focus on (Account Mapping II)

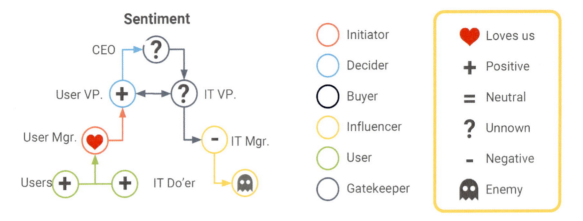

STEP 6 Orchestrate an external Account Development Plan

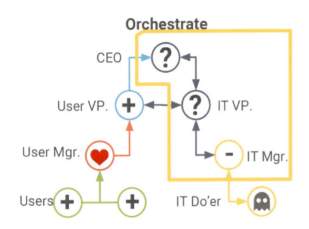

Example Action Plan

1. We will keep User Team happy by _____

2. Talk to the User VP to Identify the Impact that IT VP wants.

3. Develop a 3 x 3
   - Ask User VP for intro into IT VP.
   - Have our CEO reach out to their CEO with with an invite to introduce to "another customer CEO" on xyz.

4. Leverage our upcoming webinar on _____ and ask _____ to attend … better yet to be part of the panel.

5. Send Gartner report to ___IT Manager_____

6. Shoot a video at <customer> addressing questions of IT VP.

Example 3 x 3: **Orchestrate relationships between 3 on your side with 3 on the customer side**

Customer team	Your team
Championed by User VP	**Championed by YOU**
1. ………………customer CEO ………………	1. ……………Mark our CEO…………………
2. ……………customer VP of IT……………	2. ………Mary our VP of Eng………………
3. ……………User Manager…………………	3. ……Alex Head of Product………………

EXAMPLE Upsell

Pricing across multiple departments creates a great opportunity for a LARGE upsell that exceeds that of the "additional department."

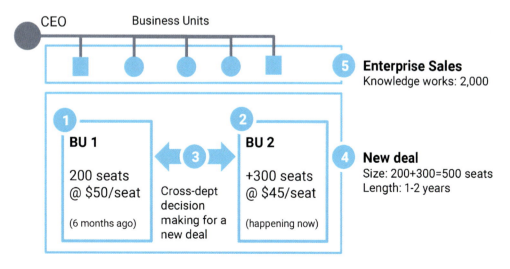

Figure 22: Departmental upselling

1. Six months ago, Business Unit 1 (BU 1) purchased 200 seats at a price of $50/user = $10,000 They have become avid users and recommend you to talk to Business Unit 2 (BU 2).

2. BU 2 has 300 users, and you find yourself in the midst of negotiating a better price – say $40/user. You want to close the deal ASAP. Deal size $12,000 (total $22,000).

3. Closing the deal at just $40 for the additional users has cross-departmental impact. Each department had its own decision process; however, when you go cross-department, you have the opportunity to increase to a new budget level from the Executive staff.

4. You can find yourself negotiating a deal for 500 users at $40/seat, with a new contract that starts NOW and has a term of 12 or even 24 months. 500 x $40 = $20,000 – $5,000 ($10,000 amortized over 6 months) = $15,000.

5. However, you now create the option to escalate the decision process to the entire Enterprise. and in some cases close a wall-to-wall enterprise deal increase 2,000 seats * $30 = $60,000 – $5,000 = $55,000.

BEST PRACTICES

- **DO** bring people together when they are ready for a decision.
- **DO NOT** bring people together to discuss problems (beyond those that are directly involved).
- **DO NOT** step into a meeting with multiple people, unprepared, thinking to yourself "I can do this."
- **DO NOT** bring in your CEO into a situation where she is put in a position to commit without prep.
- **DO** involve a specialist in your company to tackle specific issues.
- **DO NOT** be the "know it all:" It is good to defer answering a critical question. You do not have to be fluent in everything.

3. Prescribe

Prescription before diagnosis is malpractice

– Unknown

Following the diagnosis, it is time for you to demonstrate how you can help your customer. There are three very different scenarios:

SHARE
a customer story

Often used in first engagement with a customer when they ask *"what do you do?"*

SHOW
an example

Often used in follow-up engagements when a customer asks *"I want to see how it works?"*

PROVOKE
an action

Used to stop conventional thinking: *"In our estimate your current approach is costing you $10M. If you don't change you will lose x% market share in the next 12 months.*

What all of these have in common is they follow a storytelling format. The most common format in use in the business world today is explained by Simon Sinek.

EXERCISE Watch this video and apply to your company

Watch this video

goo.gl/nHEtWe

Simon Sinek
How great leaders inspire action
22M views • May 2010

Why? What is happening in the market (Aargh I have a problem)?

....

....

....

How? What is the approach to solve this (AHA a solution)?

....

....

....

What? What does your company do? (WOW what an expert)

....

....

....

EXAMPLE **Basic storyline of a customer-centric corporate presentation**

Story Stage	Description
Introduction: Get to the point!	Grab their attention with an interesting quote/tweet, and share a real life story of your experience. Add a picture! **Prepare to ask a Question.**
Why: Problem Statement	Describe why a problem is happening in the "market," sharing your market insights and, if available, market research. Again consider sharing a real life story of a customer and how they experienced the problem! **Ask a Q.**
How: Conceptual solution	How to tackle this problem, the approach, a better service etc. How would it look and feel? Do this without mentioning your company or product but rather in terms of concepts (cloud, mobile, etc.) **Ask a Q.**
What: Practical Solution	Describe a practical example of what you do to help tackle a customer's challenges. **Ask a Q.**
Proof: Customer story	Leverage a ***relevant*** use-case by a similar company/industry trying to solve the same thing. For this to be effective, it must be relevant. **Ask a Q.**
Show: Be proud/listen!	Show 1 relevant use-case for what the customer is looking to solve. **Ask a Q!**
Next Steps	**Ask** what actions to take.

BEST PRACTICES

- **DO** follow this mantra: Prepare. Practice. Reflect. Refine.
- **DO** make your opening catchy – you've got 5-15 seconds!
- **DO** exude passion, reading from a script will reduce passion.
- **DO** make it feel like it is personalized, talk to a human, in real language.
- **DO** be concise about what you do, short and to the point, as if you are talking to a 6-year-old.
- **DO** integrate customer examples into your story:
    - **DO NOT** just put their logo on the opening slide.
    - **DO** Include real pictures of their App/Service.
    - **DO** Include people and highlight statements they made. Make this a critical part of your "discovery."
        Example: "The lack of x, y and z made it impossible for him to meet deadlines."
- **DO** engage your audience meaningfully:
    Instead of: *"Questions?"*
    Try (closed): *"Does this resonate with you?", "___, do you experience something similar?"*
    Better yet (open): *"Mike can you an example of ... with me?"*
- **DO** connect the slides through story.
- **DO** speak from a customer perspective.
    Instead of: *"We are really strong at this and this... that's why customers buy us all the time"*
    Try: *"Customers similar to you... experienced exactly the same... and here is what they did."*
- **DO** use video/visuals to make the point, but make the point! Prezify your powerpoint.

- **DO** record your own presentation (just the audio by itself is already good). Listen, learn, and improve it, then do it again. I realize you find it awkward to listen to yourself; no worries, that will be gone by the 26th time. Quicktime is a simple way to do this.

3.1 Share a Customer Story

The use of use-cases as a third-party reference drastically helps your storytelling. In the example below, you notice the hard pitch – followed by the rejection. This can put a quick stop to a conversation. Do this 2-3 times and you'll see that your pitch is rendered pretty much useless.

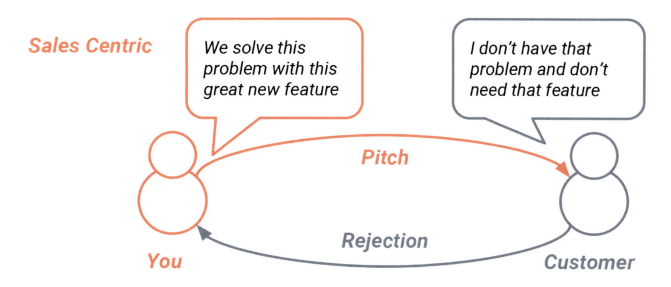

Figure 23: Sales-centric by pitching a customer

How direct pitching causes issues

Using a 3rd-party reference through storytelling can make all the difference:

- Does not fatigue as fast (e.g., you can run multiple examples).
- Provides value with your statement (e.g., how others do this).
- Makes you come across as an expert (e.g., you know people, understand their situation).

How a 3rd-party reference can have an impact

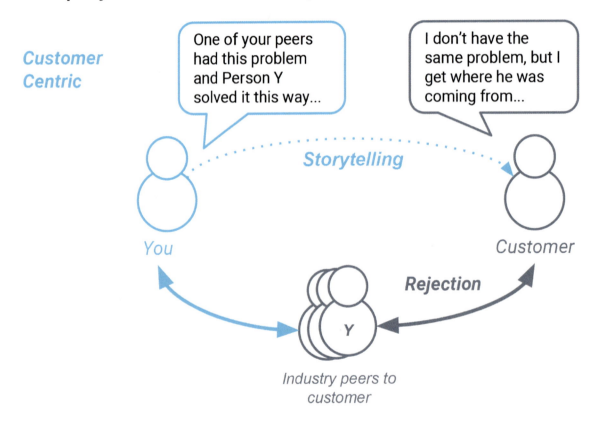

Figure 24: Customer-centric by using a customer story

When you use a 3rd-party reference, you talk through: Who experienced the problem (person), what was the problem they experienced (in context), what action did they take, what was the result they got from it, what did they learned from it, and how they applied it.

EXAMPLE **Storytelling**

Mark was a new VP of Sales, and he had recently hired a team of new SDRs. And he wanted them to be the world's best SDRs. But Mark's problem was that his team was new and untrained, and to make matters worse they were distributed all across the country.

He needed a trainer that would be part of his team's DNA, and was comfortable and effective working with remote teams. So, Mark contracted a company that offered online training, with recurring weekly drill programs and detailed playbooks, that used a train-the-trainer model.

After implementing this training program, Mark noticed improvements across the board: The number of SQLs went up – but what he had not anticipated was that they started to close faster. He started to realize that the AEs could also benefit from the same training. Today Mark applies the same training to the entire team, which includes the customer success managers (CSMs).

On the next page, we describe how to use storytelling using the "PARLA" (Problem, Action, Result, Learnings, Applied) approach.

Company	Person	'Parla'
ORIO	Mark a new VP of Sales, just hired 6 SDRs in addition to 4 AEs	*Description:* Recently hired a team of new-to-the-job SDRs and wanted them to be the world's best SDRs. *Problem:* Untrained and all across the country. *Action:* Bring in a training company that offered: - Online training - Recurring weekly drill programs - Detailed playbook - Homework to practice - Used a train-the-trainer model *Result/Impact:* Impact it has made across the board. - Increase in SQLs - Shorter sales cycle *Learnings:* His AEs can benefit from this as well. *Applied:* The same training methodology is now applied to the team of AEs.

EXERCISE Create a use-case story

Company	Person	'Parla'
....	....	*Description:* .... *Problem:* .... *Action:* .... *Result/Impact:* .... *Learnings:* .... *Applied:* . ...

3.2 Show/Demo

> Say what you are going to say. Say it. Then tell them what you've said.
>
> – Dale Carnegie

This will be described in 2 parts:

- Part 1: Key principles of demonstrating your product.
- Part 2: How to integrate this into a 15/0/60 minute meeting.

Let's start at the beginning.

Part 1: Demonstrate your product

Following the diagnosis, you identified 3 key value points (A), (B), and (C). You have prescribed your customer a solution to their problem – for example, "it needs to be cloud-based, provide detailed analytics for managers and users, and it should be simple to use."

The customer is eager to see all this in action – and so the time has come for you to perform a demonstration of your platform.

By far, the number one challenge for sales professionals is that this turns into a monologue that can last anywhere from 10-40 minutes and is lovingly known by sales professionals as the "sh!t show."

The problem is that you will overwhelm the customer – fatiguing the customer with an onslaught of your pitch. You are doing this for the fourth time that day. This is their first. And so they lose interest when there is too much information that they can relate back to their circumstance.

And with that you miss understanding some of their key challenges. The figure below shows the experience.

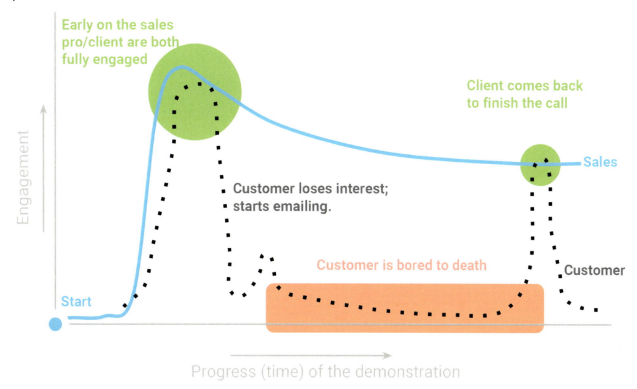

Figure 25: How a traditional demo can result in a waste of time

Instead, what you are suppose to do is "re-engage" the customer by asking questions that are related to the specific things you learned during the diagnosis.

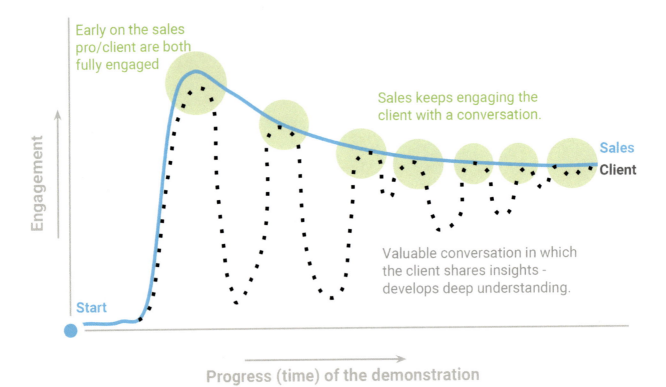

Figure 26: How to perform an engaging demo

How to engage a customer?

STEP 1 **Demonstrate your product in their context**

Before we get started, I'd like to confirm that your top challenges are {challenge 1, and challenge 2}, and you're looking for {their desired solution}. Did I get that right?

Always try to phrase it in their words and context. Pick up on how they speak about their customers and products.

STEP 2 **Describe the layout of the screen**

What you see on this screen are 4 different panes each with a different use-case; we are not going to worry about [X], [Y] and [Z]

Feel free to point out what they should NOT be focused on as well.

STEP 3 **Always discuss why you are showing a particular page, dashboard or feature**

Your customer will likely need to sell this internally to their team. Make sure your story relates to them with anecdotes that will be easier to share. You want your customer after the call to say something like: "They have something that will let us gain visibility into this process that ultimately helps solve "Challenge 1."

STEP 4 **Summarize your previous diagnosis and key customer pain**

Then briefly familiarize your customer with the layout on the screen – Let them know what the different panes mean without going into detail. You've got 5-10 seconds max to do this.

Based on our previous conversations with your team, your top priority is to solve [Challenge 1] and are also interested in [2]. Did I get that right?

Yes, exactly. We also care about [3]

Ok, thank you. Based on your priorities, I would like to cover only the relevant parts of our solution that will help you.

STEP 5 **Then, in context of the customer, demonstrate how your product solves their problem**

Avoid the temptation to show them every feature and potential solution of your solution.

The top-performing sales organizations only show their solution after discovery, then customize what they show to only the customer's top challenges.

Buyers don't care about your solution. They care about removing the roadblocks to accomplishing their objectives and to be more successful.

Because you are looking to solve [1], this particular dashboard shows the insight your management team will use to make decisions and meet your business goals.

STEP 6 Ask if what you showed was relevant, or helpful.

Can you see yourself using this service?
What stands out most to you on this page that would help your team?

STEP 7 Upon their response, immediately diagnose the situation

Can you see yourself using this service?
Yes – this is exactly what we are looking for.
What would the impact be if you had this today?

Keep engaging the customer asking for feedback.

Involve the customer. It's easy when discussing something you're passionate about to barely take time to take a breath. Make sure to pepper your conversation with questions to make sure it is relevant to the customer.

Does that resonate with you?
What part of what I've just showed you seems like it would be the best help?

STEP 8 **Hand over controls. Let them test drive!**

Customers love to feel in control. Let them be the judge, and once you've given them the fundamental high-level overview of your customized solution, ask them to give it a spin.

> *Based on what you see on my screen, is there anything you'd like to click on or dive more deeply into?*

STEP 9 **Summarize and move to the next point**

> *Before I move on to the next point; Is there anything else we have forgotten that is important to address? So in summary... you have this problem... and as you can see this would help you solve [ABC] Resulting in [this] impact on your business.*
>
> *Now let's talk about the next point...*

STEP 10 **Rinse and repeat**

Rinse and repeat for other points. Throughout the demo, make sure you continue to refine your understanding of the customer's situation, problem and desired outcomes.

Customers are often shown every little thing your company can do, or are told about this cool new feature coming out soon. Focus just on what's on the truck today, and what is most relevant for your customer. Keep doing this for every part (tab-page) of the demonstration.

 **PRO TIP** Turn on your video camera to "put a face to the voice" and ask your customer to do the same. Because they are on camera, they are more likely to stay engaged which maximizes both of your time, and maybe even lets the call end early.

- JACCO VAN DER KOOIJ

EXERCISE Create a Storyboard

Key Moments	Speaking Points
Outline	Three key things I will show you today are: 1. .... 2. .... 3. ....
#1 Feature	Show 1: .... You earlier said: .... Customer impact story: .... Impact: ....

Key Moments	Speaking Points
#2 Feature	Show 2: ....
	You earlier said: ....
	Customer impact story: ....
	Impact: ....
#3 Feature	Show 3: ....
	You earlier said: ....
	Customer impact story: ....
	Impact: ....
Close	Today I showed three things:
	6. .... ➜ Impact on your business
	7. .... ➜ Impact on your business
	8. .... ➜ Impact on your business
	Next steps...

Part 2: Integrate the demonstration into the call

We now need to integrate this world class demo into an overall structure. This can be seen below.

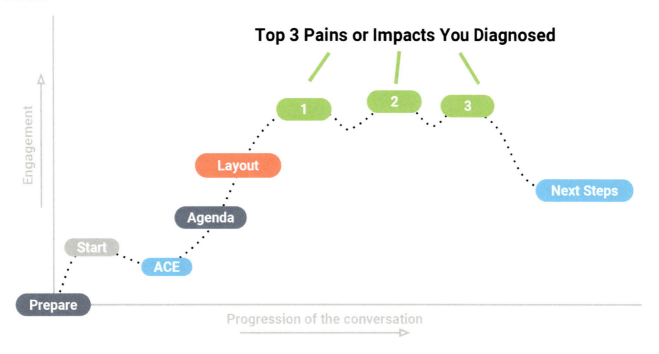

Figure 27: Integrating the demo in the meeting structure

Prepare for the meeting.

Goal: Review the key points of the diagnosis and match to your demonstration.

Before even getting on the call, you have set up the meeting as a professional: Executive briefing, reminders, technology check, and a clear understanding of your desired outcome of the call.

Start the conversation

Goal: Set yourself up as a friendly professional, and exchange warm business friendly pleasantries as you get started.

Show that you've done your research as people join the call – ask about a relevant news article or key milestone that could be important to the individual (work anniversary, product release, recent funding, etc.).

Mike, during the diagnosis call you said you experienced problems with ____ , ____ and ____ did I get that right?

Yes that's right.

Well today, I'd like to demonstrate step-by-step how this can be solved.

NOTE: If there are 2-4 people on the call, let them briefly introduce themselves. If there are lots of people on the call, run it through your coach.

ACE your meeting

Confirm your agenda

I have planned to cover [Agenda written in invite]. Mrs. Decision Maker, what would you like to get out of our call today?

Sure I'd like to see … and …

Yes, I will make sure we have time to cover this in the demonstration.

Demonstration of [1], [2], and [3] as detailed previously
Next Steps
During the ACE, you set the stage for the outcome of a successful demo. During the demo you earned their follow-up. Now this is the time to ask for it!

At the beginning of the call we discussed that a successful demo today would lead to next steps.

Are you pleased with what has been demonstrated today?

Yes. This was a great demo!

Thank you! We worked hard on it.
May I ask if you are ready to move forward with a proposal?

3.3 Provoke/Challenge

When to use provocative selling

Only to a handful of identified accounts, which are handpicked because:

- There is a high (>50%) chance of impacting their business.
- We understand the problem the customer faces.
- We have identified a critical event.
- We can access to customers senior executives.

Key traits
- **Prepare** – Detailed preparation of the technical, economical, and political environment. Has a thorough emotional understanding of the decision maker. Must be able to tailor their value proposition to resonate with the decision-maker's hot-button issues.

- **Educate** – Can go to the whiteboard and provide insights tailored to a customer's needs, the problem/solution, and value behind the provocative value prop. Show the customer a new approach on how to compete in their market.

- **Provoke** – Identifying an impact and creating a critical event that leads to immediate action. Is not afraid of a professional confrontation on a topic, but must be able to back it up with research.

- **Storytelling** – Must be able to share stories of other persons in the same situation better, yet stories from within the identified company.

And the most critical one of all:

- **Orchestrate** -Organize all the company's resource to achieve the anticipated result on-time.

How to provoke

Phase 1: Identify

STEP 1 Identify 3 accounts based on **ICE** use an existing relationship of a recent win.

Key Account	Impact	Critical Event	Similar Recent Win
....			
....			
....			

STEP 2 **Research.** Use the SDR team to develop deep insights on these 3 accounts. Get to know your customers' world better than they do. This allows you to teach them what they should know but don't know. What data, information, or insight can you put in front of your customer that reframes the way they think about their business—how they operate.

- 10K/10Q statements
- Videos of the CEO on YouTube
- Press release/blog posts/tweets

STEP 3 **Orchestrate –** The biggest differentiator is the amount of time you spend planning. You've got to build a network of advocacy along the way or risk losing the deal altogether, due to weak support across the organization. Marketing must serve as the "insight-generation machine" that keeps you well-equipped with materials your customers will find compelling.

Action: Orchestrate based on the following questions:

- What are we going to communicate with them on? Value proposition (Impact, etc.)
- Who do we need to talk to first, second and third?
- Where do we need to talk them (channel, tradeshow, visit etc.)?

Phase 2: Diagnose

STEP 4 **Outreach to start a conversation.** Be relevant to them! Leverage your research and get to the point.

Action: Work together with the SDR to create a target campaign. Consider use of an existing customer sponsor for example to create an intro.

STEP 5 **Have the conversation –** Build credibility and show your prospect you understand their challenges. This serves as the introduction for the pitch. By helping customers think differently about their company, you ultimately want them to think differently about your company. Instead of asking, **Who needs to be involved?** You have to coach your customer on who should be involved.

Action: Prepare insights you going to share to anchor your conversation.

STEP 6 **Diagnose –** Find value! Identify critical event and impact. Figure below outlines most common areas of finding value.

Action: Highlight in the picture below what the CEO has expressed the most about!

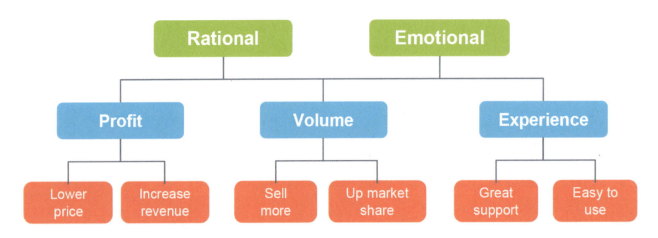

Figure 29: Circle the C-suite's most important values

Phase 3: Select

STEP 7 **Vision Pitch.** What sets us apart is not the quality of our products, but the value of our insights — give them new ideas to help customers either make money or save money in ways they didn't even know were possible.

Action: Create a vision pitch with new relevant ideas for their business.

82 – The SaaS Sales Method for Account Executives

STEP 8 **Workshop.** Goal is to reframe the challenges to a bigger problem or opportunity they hadn't previously considered *AND that you have prepared your company for to solve*. Build credibility by showing your customer you understand their challenges.

Action: Which expert are you going to bring in/fly in/conference in to share their insights.

Phase 4: Provoke

STEP 9 **Provoke** your customer with new perspectives, specifically tailored to their most-pressing business needs, in a compelling and assertive enough manner to ensure that the message not only resonates, but actually drives action. Show prospects the numbers behind why they should think differently with a provocative statement, help them identify new opportunities to cut costs, increase revenue, penetrate new markets, and mitigate risk in ways they themselves have not yet recognized.

> **EXAMPLE** **Provocative Statement**
>
> "In our estimate, your current approach is costing you $10M/year. If you don't change, you will lose 12% market share in the next 12 months."

Action: What does the provocative statement sound like: ....

Current approach cost: ....

New approach brings you: ....

Loss of market share: ....

Create the provocative statement: ....

....

....

PRO TIP I've found over the years that customers will repay me with loyalty when I have taught them something they valued. Note, teaching them something that helps them reframe a problem supersedes selling them something they need.

- JACCO VAN DER KOOIJ

STEP 10 **Business Case:** A good ROI calculator calculates the ROI on solving the challenge you've just taught your customer they have, not the ROI on buying your solution. Shift the discussion from price to value.

Action: Make the business case:

Customer pays us: ....

Customer gets: ....

STEP 11 **Showcase** why your way of thinking about the solution is the right way, and how it fits with the new way your customers should be thinking about their business.

Action: Which reference customer will you fly them into? What will you demonstrate? Why?

Phase 5: Proof

STEP 12 **Proof:** Present Emotional Impact, then create an emotional connection between the pain in the story you're telling and the pain they feel every day in their organization.

Action: Present a series of quotes from real stories from people within the company that you have spoken to and that you kept. Put all those quotes together to tell a story that bolsters your provocative statement and business case!

STEP 13 **Verify:** They have discovered a new way make sure you keep the speed up. Get all your paperwork prepared. They are hungry for results – this cannot be held up for months.

Action: What are the most common hold-ups and remedies

Hold-up	Remedy

Phase 6: Trade

STEP 14 **Negotiate** stop negotiating and start trading with.

Action: Create a trade-off matrix (see section 6.7)

STEP 15 **Attain commitment**

Action: Execute the step by step action plan you orchestrated together with the executive team.

3.4 Handling Objections

Across customers there are a few common objections. A customer raising an objection is them expressing the interest to buy. And guess what? 95% of objections are alike. That means we as experts can say the source of the mentioned objection often is 4-5 layers deep. This requires a deep understanding of question-based techniques to uncover the real objection – in particular, the "Value style" questions.

Variety of objections

Not every objection is the same – here are the most common categories:

Type of Objection	What They Say	What It Tells You
Lack of understanding the value	"We don't need that"	Establish value by asking questions on the impact on their business. Keep asking.
Raising a concern	"Your product is too complicated"	Show that this is not the case. Literally SHOW them, and let them DO IT. You can't write/talk your way out of this.
Wrong perception	"That does not pass our security profile"	Need to provide proof of how others overcame that issue.
Lack of priority	"That feature you offer is not a priority"	Establish impact of that feature, and present it back to them … e.g., this feature means less training.
Unclear about the decision process	"That costs as much as our entire marketing budget"	You need to sell at a higher level. Use organizational selling to get execs involved.
Secret agenda	The VP worked with your competitor at a previous company and appears to want to use them again	Research beforehand. Need to flush this out in the disco call and ask "what did you not like working with…" You need to learn if this is a (+) or (-) impact. If (-) you need to apply organizational selling.

Objection handling – How it works

STEP 1 Prepare BEFORE you get on the call

STEP 2 Ask and perform Active Listening

STEP 3 Summarize and appreciate *"Did I understand correctly that..."*

"Thank you for raising the concern."

STEP 4 Empathize *"We hear this a lot"*

STEP 5 Get the whole picture (tipping the bucket) *"Is there anything else?"*

STEP 6 Summarize and appreciate *"If I may summarize... did I get that right?"*

STEP 7 Ask questions to uncover the real needs

STEP 8 Counter-offer based on what is important to them

You may have noticed that Step 3 and Step 6 are similar. This is because you must listen intently and confirm you understand exactly what they are objecting to or asking for. The risk for assuming their objection is similar to your last customer is too high – and will often cause you to try and compromise on the wrong trigger.

Understand / Peer reference / Solution they found

- Confirm you listened *"I **understand** you are experiencing..."*
- Show empathy *"Your **peers** experienced exactly the same thing"*
- Make a 3rd-party reference *"The **solution** they found was..."*

EXERCISE Objection Handling

STEP 1 Identify the most common objections (in this stage)

- ....
- ....

STEP 2 Pick an objection

- ....

STEP 3 Ask diagnostic questions

- ....
- ....

STEP 4 Identify others who had the same objection

- ....
- ....

STEP 5 Offer stats/proof that you learned from existing customers

- ....
- ....

STEP 6 Address concerns

- *I understand how you feel about that* ....
- *Others such as* .... *and* .... *felt the same way* ....
- *What they found was that* .... *and as a result* ....

4 Select

4.1 Determine Decision Criteria

The decision criteria are like the four center squares of a chess board. Control them, and your chances of winning the game radically increase. This is why it is so important to get engaged with a customer early on in the sales process. With early involvement, you are able to set the stage and control the decision criteria.

STEP 1 Use a basic matrix like the one below to establish the customer's key decision criteria.

- During the first call/engagement, it is key for you to inquire about the customer's decision criteria, and inform your AE during the transfer.

- In the opening call, verify these decision criteria with your customer. In the process, try to identify the competitors they are looking at.

Figure 29: Decision criteria vs. other options (competitors, substitutes, status quo)

STEP 2 **Prioritize**

Now the AE verifies with the customer the decision criteria and asks *"is this the right priority?"* This way, we can figure out what is most important. Next, using a variety of exchanges, it is up to the AE to establish where we are in the deal on each of these criteria. How do we stack up – are we first, second or third?

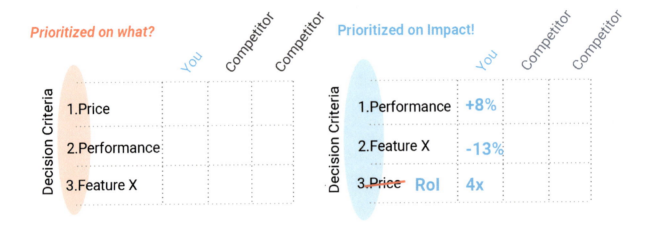

Figure 30: Decision criteria prioritized

 **NOTE:** During the call/meeting a customer's says *"I am looking at you and several competitors."* Most sales people will jump the gun by asking *"May I ask who are the competitors you are looking at?* The better approach is to focus on the decision criteria: *"May I ask what factors will affect your choice?"*

Sales Centric:
Who do we compete with?

Customer Centric:
What are your decision criteria?

STEP 3 **Figure out "where we are" in the deal**

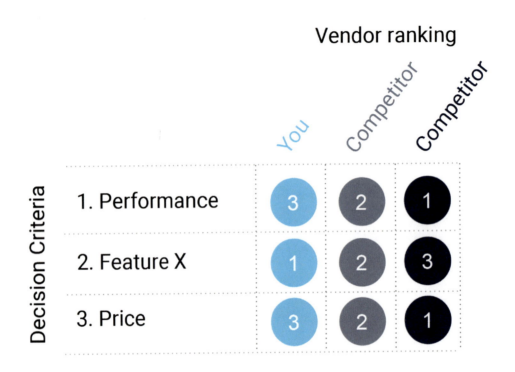

Figure 31: Taking inventory on the situation ("you" are probably ranked 3rd)

 **NOTE:** *Realize this is not easy! This is however a key task for the sales professional to determine. You can leverage your* **SPI** *question techniques to derive this during conversations with your customer.*

EXERCISE **Decision criteria**

Pick a real customer scenario, in which you are currently experiencing competition, and one in which you have reasonable insights.

STEP 1 **Determine decision criteria**

STEP 2 **Prioritize decision criteria**

Customer's Decision Criteria *In Order Of Priority*	Determine ranking		
	You	Competitor #1	Competitor #2
Criteria 1:			
Criteria 2:			
Criteria 3:			

STEP 3 **Determine ranking as best as you can today**

4.2 Prioritize on Impact

STEP 1 **Reprioritize decision criteria**

Now you need to increase the priority of what is important to the customer (impact on their business) and what you are good at. And at the same time, you need to decrease the importance of what we are not good at. In this example, we are ranked #1 on FEATURE X because it makes the most impact on the customer's business. This requires a lot of skills and techniques explained throughout the playbook, such as:

- **SPI** Question-Based Selling
- Critical Event Timeline
- Decision Process

Figure 32: Reprioritize based on impact

STEP 2 **Add decision criteria**

Obviously, we do not have to stay within the box that was drawn for us. We can add criteria important to the customer. Perhaps a feature that only we offer – say, "simple to use."

In this example, the AE must provide the customer insights that, if it is not simple to use, that the adoption of the service will falter, and waste the entire investment. The AE can provide use-cases, do demonstrations, and even set up references on this single item to make sure this gets to be THE MOST important priority.

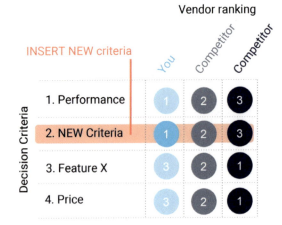

Figure 33: Insert a new criteria

NOTE: *Doing this successfully will allow you to help the customer implement the right solution AND provide you with a deal.*

STEP 3 Improve ranking

In this example, while price remains the #4 priority, it is the AE's responsibility to move his solution from a #3 ranking to a #2 ranking.

How? This can be achieved by offering the customer deeper insights, statistics, demonstrations, use-cases, reference calls with other users, etc. The outcome of this process is that the customer has a better understanding of what the right solution looks like.

Figure 34: Improve ranking

NOTE: *It is key to be persistent on this matter. Too often, an AE will think too lightly about his own solution, and think that the competitor's is perfect. All too often, all vendors are in a similar boat, and the confidence and persistence of the AE becomes the key differentiator.*

EXERCISE Decision criteria

Use the previous customer scenario and determine the impact each criteria is making (see 2.2).

Customer's Decision Criteria *In Priority Order*	Your Impact	Competitor Impact	Competitor Impact
Criteria 1:			
Criteria 2:			
Criteria 3:			

STEP 1 Add/increase priority of existing decision criteria that are in our favor:

Criteria: ....

Determine impact: ....

Determine value of impact: ....

STEP 2 Remove/decrease priority of existing decision criteria:

Criteria: ....

Determine impact: ....

Determine value of impact: ....

STEP 3 **Add a new criteria:** ....

Determine impact: ....

Determine value of impact: ....

Who is the specialist (e.g. the CFO): ....

How can you involve this person in the decision process? ....

....

Show the customer the trade-offs and help them visualize their evaluation. Build it with them on a screen share. You become a trusted consultant to help them solve their business need, while simultaneously avoiding being a pushy salesperson.

EXERCISE **Establish a tactical plan for qualified deals**
Using the information you learned up to this point to review with your team the following on all key opportunities for this month/quarter.

Tactical plan for enterprise deals
For each account, the AE must identify and establish the following key elements to achieve success:

- Understand if there is (or else create) a **critical event timeline.**

- Understand in detail the **impact of each criteria.**
- Understand in detail the **decision criteria.**
- Identify the **decision makers** – per the decision criteria.
- Determine the **decision process.**

Figure 35: Basis of a tactical plan to compete

Based on these elements, an accomplished AE can determine the appropriate sales tactic to use:

- Make performance the most important criteria.

- Make FEATURE X the least important.

- Add a new criteria that outperforms the competitor.

- Try to win on every criteria *(this is primarily where most sales professionals focus on)*

 PRO TIP Setting a sales tactic is not something that happens once. It is a fluid process that can change with each twist and turn a deal makes in response to new decision makers getting involved, your competitor adjusting to your positioning, and the ever-changing setting of priorities.

JACCO VAN DER KOOIJJ

4.3 Compete

Most products don't have 100% market share, so competitive pressures can make it seem that price is the only thing that matters. That's why you have focused your early conversations on diagnosis. Now, it's time to assist the customer with trade offs, because you know what they care about.

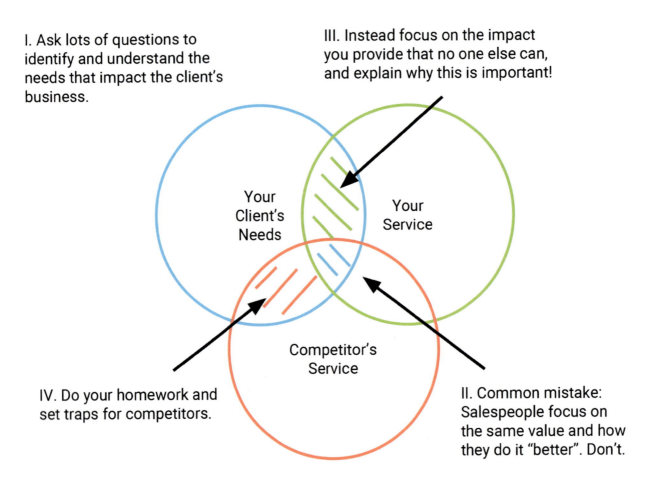

Figure 36: The basics of effective competing with competitors during the selection process

STEP 7 **Compete for the business:** Your primary focus must be on uncovering the customer's needs and identifying the ways your offering can help them with real and measurable impact on their business. So keep on asking the right questions and you will learn more and more. That knowledge will lead you in the right direction. NOT addressing customers needs will make the customer feel you are not knowledgeable, coy, or simply incapable.

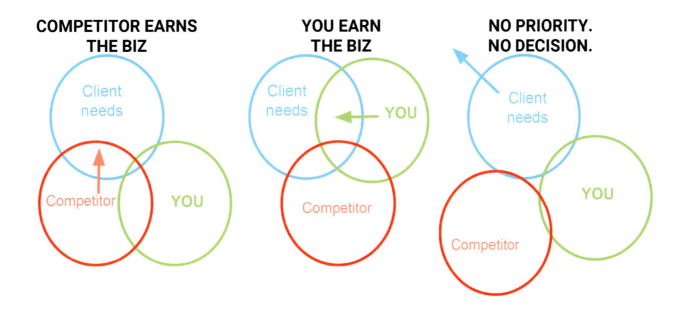

Figure 37: Basics of competing – Focus on your goal: meeting the customer's needs

NOTE: Traditionally, salespeople were very focused on competing with a competitor. They focused on what they had in common – and it ended up in a "we do this better then them" conversation. Don't. The customer will quickly come to the conclusion that "You all look alike" and it turns into a price discussion. Hence, the importance of focusing on the value this offers for the customer.

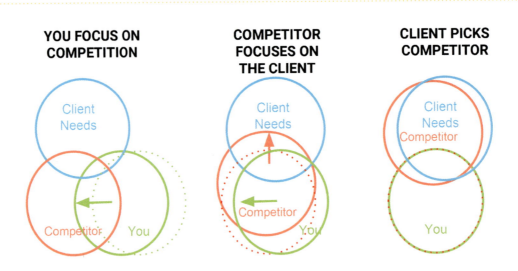

Figure 37: What happens if you focus on the competition

In the past it was considered Sales 101 not to discuss the competition, because we relied on the lack of information a customer had. No need to give them a name of a competitor they did not know about, right? Today, the customer can simply type in "competitor to [your product]" and (s)he gets a nice list of competitors to go check out. So you must focus on "placing mines" by anticipating how the competitor will position themselves. Place a mine by making that positioning a non-important decision criteria.

1. In your positioning, focus on the area of needs that you can help impact!

AE RESPONSIBILITY #1 **Knowledge**

1. You must have an intimate understanding of your customer's needs/decision criteria.
2. You must understand how your product can meet that demand, today and in the future.
3. You must learn and understand your competitors strengths and their approach.

AE RESPONSIBILITY #2 **Assist the selection process**

1. Establish the customer needs/decision criteria from the first interaction with a customer, and along the entire journey.

2. Write these decision criteria down, repeat them to the customer, and make sure you capture the exact words they use.

3. Ask the customer to prioritize these criteria (it's effective to do this visually on a screen share), and capture the implied need of each of the criteria.

4. Change the decision criteria, based on what the customer's needs are, but in favor or our service, by:

- Moving the decision criteria that favor you up in priority.
- Moving the decision criteria that favor your competitor down in priority.
- Add decision criteria that favor you, by:
    - Changing the decision process.
    - Changing the decision makers.
    - Changing the sense of urgency.
- Improve your rank (such as creating a 3-year ROI vs. 1-year pricing).

AE RESPONSIBILITY #3 **Trade-off**

- Create a trade-off matrix (next paragraphs)

BEST PRACTICES

- **DO** determine the customer needs (decision criteria)
- **DO** determine the impact of those needs on their business.
- **DO** determine the impact of that on your coach and the people you work with.
- **DO** determine who the competitors are.
- **DO** have a conversation on the details of this competitor, ask "Are you looking at others?"
- **DO** use the words "substitutes" when identifying other ways to spend their budget, and alternatives; minimize the use of the words competitors.
- **DO NOT** introduce a competitor if you do not know the above 3 points about that competitor.
- **DO**: Bringing up a known competitor early in the conversation allows you to place "mines." (see the green in the first chart of this section). These are areas where you educate the customer on questions to ask your competitor about – questions that you know will impact the decision in your favor.
- **DO NOT:** The most common mistake of salespeople is to focus on the overlap (see red + white overlap area in first chart in this section) – this turns it into a feature war.
- **DO** Instead, the key is to focus on the area where you have identified a customer's key needs that the competitor can't meet, and stay focused on this area with value propositions and use-case examples (third party validation).
- In case the competitor is an incumbent:
    - **DO** focus on what the customer was promised (red in the first chart above), and what they did not deliver on (for example, stability of the service). Provide third party proof that we can provide that.
    - **DO** combine this with teasing them new functionality that meets their needs today/future (blue area).

- **DO** ask great questions such as:

    "What made you fall in love with [your existing provider]?"

    "How is that working out for you?"

    "If there is one thing that is causing you issues with [your existing provider], what is it?"

- **DO** be:
    - Consultative. Don't tell, but ask, refer and provide info.
    - Knowledgeable. Knowledge wins every time.
    - Non-emotional (emotion = loss of composure).
    - A sincere trusted insider (and don't fake it --- truly be one!).

4.3 Strategy

The AE needs to keep close track over time how the decision matrix evolves.

In this example, we see the following three evolutions:

1. We start with a 3-criteria and 3-competitor matrix. We fill in the positioning.

2. Re-prioritize the decision criteria.

    a. Add a new criteria (A), as a result eliminate a competitor, AND

    b. eliminate Z as a key decision criteria.

3. Take another look at the decision criteria matrix... who's on top now?

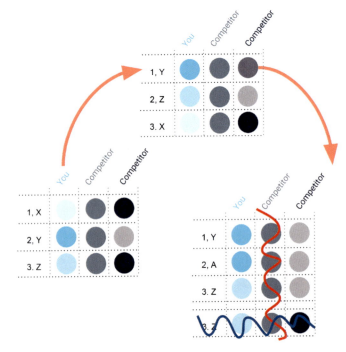

Figure 39 Orchestrating success using profiling

That is how a major deal is won! Once we establish this as a pattern for when we compete with XYZ, we can then anticipate.

5   Propose a Solution

Customers always want the best price and discounts are often a way to show commitment to helping your customer. But we do not want you to give discounts. This requires you to embrace a new way of discussing pricing and instead consider it trading.

In this case we are using a screen share to help navigate.

Establish price

STEP 1 Open a screen share or share a document so both parties are seeing the same thing.

STEP 2 Create a spreadsheet to build the proposal.

STEP 3 Enter the details of the deal: Calculate the discount over the length of the contract.

STEP 4 Do not discount any of the prices; instead make a price adjustment and note conditions.

STEP 5 Share it with the customer (as in make sure they have access) – let them play around with it.

STEP 6 If they change the number – say *"That's OK, but that changes the deal."*

Packages	Monthly Pricing	Annual Pricing	Proposed
INSTALLATION FEE	$5,500	$5,500	$5,500
USER FEE			
SMALL PACKAGE	$500	$5,500	
MEDIUM PACKAGE	**$695**	**$7,500**	$7,500
LARGE PACKAGE	$899	$9,500	
CONTRACT TERM	12 months	12 months	
PAYMENT TERMS	Upfront per month	Upfront per year	
		Sub-total	**$13,000**
		Price Adjustment*	$3,000
		Total	**$10,000**

NOTE **In return for the price adjustment corporation offers:**

- Contract by June 24, after that adjustment is null and void.
- Provide a video case study.
- Use of Logo on our website.

Create a trade-off

During the preparation, you determine through research and discussion the different variables of the deal. In this example, there are three variables; Price (ACV), Contract Term, and Onboarding Fee (installation payment).

Based on these variables, you create three deals, as visualized in this chart:

- Deal 1: 12-month contract with an ACV of $7,200, paid upfront quarterly.
- Deal 2: 24-month contract with an ACV of $6,500, paid upfront every 6 months.
- Deal 3: 36-month contract with an ACV of $5,800, paid upfront annually.

The visualization of this information allows you help the customer understand the options, and therefore more easily negotiate. And as discounts alter, so does the deal.

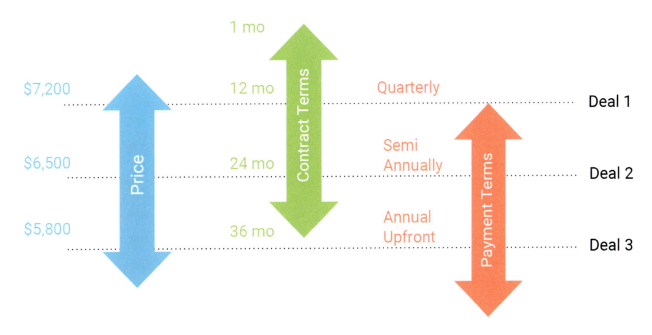

Figure 40: Trade-off visualization with three variables

Other variables to consider differ across businesses, but think of: Payment Terms (Net 30 days, N45, N60), onboarding cost, training, templates, storage space, number of seats, usage limits, and so on.

Presenting the trade-off

There are many ways of presenting the trade-off to a customer. We discuss the following

Minimum Contents	Quote	Proposal	Impact Proposal
Price	Yes	Yes	Yes
Terms	Yes	Yes	Yes
Expiration	Yes	Yes	Yes
Needs outlined		Yes	Yes
Competitor Overview		Sometimes	Yes
Critical Event Timeline		Yes	Yes
Impact on the company		Yes	Yes
Impact per role/department		Sometimes	Yes
Next steps		Yes	Yes
Annex with meeting notes		Yes	Yes
ROI Calculation			Yes

In the case of a proposal, you open a Google shared doc and start capturing each point as they are brought up. To give an idea (Minimal requirements):

- **Quote: ACV ~ $5,000** deal can have about 1-2 pages describing what, when, and who is going to do what. Followed by a 1-page quote. We strongly recommend that you included a "competitor" comparison. In case your customer is likely to take no action, we would also recommend including "no action"

- **Proposal: ACV ~ $12,000** deal has become a 5-20 page proposal, clearly outlining the full program, including lots of examples (screenshots) of how you are looking to address their needs.

    EXAMPLE **Outline**
    - Executive summary:
        - Problem you are solving and how
        - Basic outline of the offer
        - Competitor matrix
        - Next steps
    - Solution to your problem – Overview of your solution, often pictorial.
    - Your product requirements – specific needs described and how you address them.
    - Your service requirements – 24/7?
    - Your timeline – reverse chronological order timeline that starts with customer deliverable.
    - Pricing – price, expiration date, terms, reference number etc.
    - Why us? Ten reasons why you should partner with ___.
    - Next steps. Outline of the 3-4 next steps that need to be taken.

    Annex: Meeting minutes, diagrams, slides, case studies etc.

- **Value Proposal (Start) ACV = $24,000+** deal has become a 20-page proposal, outlining how you are looking to address their needs of the company. This is now turning into a value proposal and includes an ROI calculation for the CFO.

- **Value Proposal (Major) ACV = $60,000+** deal has become a 50-page proposal, outlining how you are looking to address the needs of individual groups within the company. This is now turning into a value proposal and includes an ROI calculation for each department.

5.1 Quote

Every quote should be standardized. You cannot make your own quote. Here is an outline of the minimum information that needs to be on your quote.

EXAMPLE

1 Every quote must have an expiration date.

2 Reference is needed for invoices later on.

3 Note "price adjustment"
NOT discount Don't zero out products that are discounted, as these discounts may not apply to subsequent years.

4 Mention specifically what you negotiated to have in return for the price adjustment.

5 Start at a minimum the renewal for next year. This is needed to make sure that you do not have to extend year 1 discount into future years.

6 Include terms. At a minimum, payment terms and the conditions of sale (ownership).

5.2 Impact Proposal

A solid proposal makes ALL the difference. For smaller deals that may be a professional-looking quote, and for larger deals, it will be a multi-page proposal. The proposal helps outline the work you have done till date and represents the customer's needs/challenges and your plan to help them with it.

What is the difference between a value proposal and an impact proposal? The picture below shows that an impact proposal also looks at usage to create the impact desired.

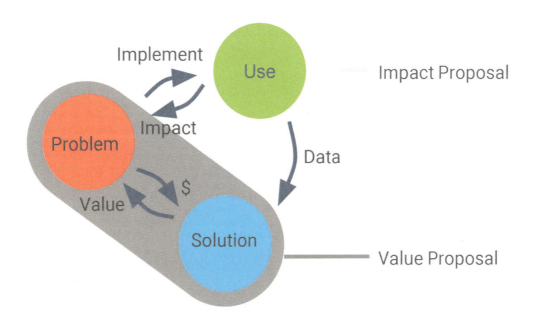

Figure 42: Value proposal vs. impact proposal

EXAMPLE of an impact proposal

PART 1 **Executive briefing –** This includes a professional headshot of you, and a brief Why/How/ What including a vision of the company. The goal of this briefing is to assist in the development of your proposal.

PART 2 **Value proposition –** A simplified value prop that outlines the desired outcome:
- The problem your company was approached with
- The key value points discussed

- The goals you are looking to accomplish with the service

PART 3 **Customer pain points** – Specific descriptions of their pain points. Keep it short.

PART 4 **Impact on the business** – Demonstrate the negative impact of these pain points on their business. There are three key areas to focus on; 1) Improve growth, 2) reduce costs, 3) improve user experience. The key reason you lose deals is the lack of priority, NOT budget NOR competitors.

PART 5 **Examples** – Provide real practical examples.

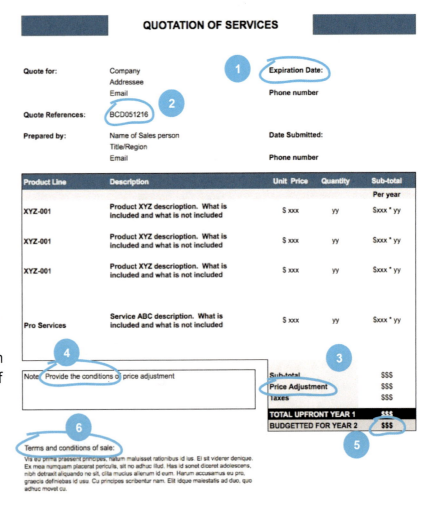

Figure 41: Example quote

PART 6 **Plan** – Describe in bullets what are we going to do to fix this problem.

PART 7 **Deliverables** – An outline of deliverables, where possible provide a visual example. Agree to a series of Key Performance Indicators of success (and also what failure looks like).

PART 8 **Who is involved** – A list of people who will be involved, their contact data, and the role they play.

PART 9 **Timeline** – A rough outline of a timeline of activities. No need for a gantt chart.

PART 10 **Price** – Provide a pricing overview. Spend time on simplifying your offer so it can be understood without having to need a 2-day training course on your service.

PART 11 **Terms** – Clearly outline what is included, but also what is NOT included.

PART 12 **Trade-off** – Educate your customer on the Pros and Cons of your service. Educate them on the variety of decisions. The trade-off should include:

- You vs. Competitors (spend with similar solution).
- You vs. Substitutes (spend with alternative solution solving the same problem).
- Not spend – Cost of doing nothing.
- Delay – Cost of delay by day/week/month.

PART 13 **Next steps** – In a few simple bullets, outline the next steps. There are two ways of doing this: Chronological starting with the execution of the document, or reverse starting with the key deliverable. Either way, please clearly outline the deliverable date.

PART 14 **Signature page** – Provide a clear space for document execution. It sets the tone.

5.3 Creating a Business Case

What sets a value proposal apart from a proposal is:

- It presents the value your service will create for the customer, e.g. buy $1 get $5.
- It presents this either per person, per department, or per role – HR cost are $2 but they get $3.
- It calculates over a period of several years the accumulated costs vs. gains, obviously presenting an incredible return.

Your company offers a service and it is valued at an Annual Contract Value of $224,000/year. Your buyer is not experienced and is complaining this will never fit in the budget. She is indicating to you that $100,000 is the budget? You are tempted to get the approval from the manager as to why this is "only for year 1" and "we have to get in" or "this is just the start." Clearly you want to get the deal done. Your buyer is right now assisting you to get approval for the $100,000 sale.

This is the wrong way around!

The better approach for you is to determine the value proposal and to help your buyer get internal approval for the purchase. The way to do this is to make a value proposal.

EXAMPLE of a value prop

Service offered priced at $224,000.

Customer uses your service to reduce churn and improve quality of the service:

- Annual churn: 6%
- Number of customers: 600,000
- Price of the service: $39.95/year

Your impact reduces churn by 0.5%

Value proposition: 0.5% x 600,000 x $39.94 = $11,982,000

BEST PRACTICES

- **DO NOT** attach a business case as a PDF to an email unless you have to (e.g. security); if you have tracking software, send it as a link so you can monitor engagement.
- **DO** add valuable insights in the appendix of the business case.
- **DO** keep it short and to the point.
- **DO NOT** mention the word "Discount" or "Free" anywhere in your proposal. Instead refer to "price adjustment" and clearly state what you received in return for the price adjustment.
- **DO** clearly state an expiration date, and the consequence of expiration.
- **DO** clearly state in your proposal that it supersedes all previous proposals.
- **DO** add any relevant email exchange as an appendix. For example, the part where it clearly described the problem diagnosis of the customer early on.

6   Pause/Go Dark

The most common reason for losing a deal is extended delay. In order to assist a customer during the delay, you need to do three specific things:

- **DO NOT** harass them; this can often lead to the customer feeling guilty or getting annoyed, and either one is usually a huge turn-off for them.

- **DO** make sure your proposal, presentations, videos, and emails are all enabled with tracking. In case the customer reengages with your proposal – you will know when it happens and can take immediate action.

- **DO** make sure you continue to assist by providing valuable insights in a slow-drip campaign – with a focus on customer use-cases. You want to keep educating the customer with what others are doing, and the benefits they are getting.

- **DO** agree with the customer, for example:
    - Mike is the buyer; he has asked Ellie for a proposal. Mike shares with Ellie that it will take about a week before the monthly budget meeting happens where he will put forth the proposal, and then he will go out of country for another week, so it will be at least a month before he can get back to her. What do you do?

STEP 1 **Confirm with Mike on the phone and/or in email what you are doing**

{{First name}},

Please find attached a link to the proposal. As agreed, it is for 5 seats/2 months at $6,000 and it offers a 12% price adjustment if we receive the paperwork by ____. If not, the adjustment will be based on volume.

Mike, if questions arise, I am available at 123-456-7890. If I don't hear back from you by {{date}}, I will reach out on {{date}}. In the meantime, I will send along some relevant info.

Have a great trip to London!

Best,

{{Your name}}

STEP 2 Make sure your proposal has tracking enabled

STEP 3 Add Mike to your sales nurturing drip campaign

STEP 4 Remove Mike from the marketing nurture drip campaign

STEP 5 Set up the actions for what you are going to do, based on what Mike does

For example:

- If Mike opens the proposal, then you will…
- If Mike forwards the proposal, then you will…
- If Mike opens the use-cases, then you will…
- If Mike forwards the use-cases, then you will…

6.1 Set Alerts

A particular way to keep tabs on your lost customer is to set Alerts. The point of an Alert is that you stay in touch with them over the months to come. The types of triggers you set up depend per market. For example for a hyper-growth start-up we would set the following triggers

Effective alerts

- Raised a new round of funding.
- New Executive or Board Member hired.
- Moved into new office.
- Hiring more people.

Alert tools

- Google Alerts – Company name, Person name.
- IFTTT – in case of alert do this (like add link to article to a Google sheet).
- **Owler** – Follow your identified companies and competitors.
- **LinkedIn** Saved Searches (Company hiring/job openings).
- **Twitter** generated Alert (i.e. TweetDeck).
- Specific vertical portals: such as **Crunchbase** or **Mattermark** for the VC industry.

6.2 Keep Educating (FOMO)

Set up a series of articles in a queue that go out to customers that are in decision mode. Hand-pick articles that match your customer's situation – the more customized the message, the stronger the bond it creates. It essentially creates the Fear Of Missing Out (FOMO).

Just as you nurture prospects, it is important to nurture people who have delayed their decision. The best way to do this is to categorize your personas and find articles that fit the biggest pain points they are looking to solve.

Hi Maureen,

Here's an article that made me think of you based on our past conversations about solving {Value Prop 1}.

Harvard Business Review just released best practices on leveraging design thinking at scale. In particular, "The focus on great experiences isn't limited to product designers, marketers, and strategists—it infuses every customer-facing function."

Maureen, would it be valuable to share how other companies we work with like you are solving this?

Cheers,

Brandon

For example, CxOs care more about strategy and industry insights that are relevant to their business. Managers, on the other hand, are interested in things like motivating their team and leadership progression. Bucket your content into relevant cohorts. Do not send the same email to everyone.

PRO TIP Focus on providing insights that are relevant – this includes 3rd-party articles (like HBR), but also a sprinkle of relevant use-cases. Always point out the specific part in the use-case – don't just send the PDF.

- DAN SMITH

Customers make decisions emotionally first, then justify rationally. Part of what you are achieving with the FOMO approach is realizing that many people are motivated by avoiding mistakes instead of finding the absolute best solution.

BEST PRACTICES

- **DO NOT** "sell" them – focus on what's in it for them, and speaking about relevant 3rd-party experiences.
- **DO** make sure your FOMO is centered around the individual customer – help them get promoted with the insights you are sending them.
- **DO NOT** only share content branded with your company logo.
- **DO** point out the particular paragraph or insight you think is most relevant.

7 Trade

You've earned their business. After diagnosing the customer, helping them understand trade-offs and showing them a solution that solves their pain on time and within budget, it's time to seal the deal.

7.1 Trade

Although we will negotiate the deal, think of it as trading.

trad·ing
/ˈtrādiNG/
noun

the exchange of goods or services between parties

This means that we have to learn what "goods" or "services" we are going to exchange.

EXERCISE Create a list of services or goods to trade

Trade-off table

Value	Item To Trade	Impact
$ 10,000 value	Use-case video, white paper	Marketing efforts
$ 25,000 value	A personal introduction by the customer's CEO to another CxO recommending our service	Secure a new account
$ _____ value		

Value	Item To Trade	Impact
$ _____ value		
$ _____ value		
$ _____ value		
$ _____ value		
$ _____ value		
$ _____ value		
$ _____ value		
$ _____ value		
$ _____ value		

7.2 Negotiate

As you try to achieve your goal during negotiation, you will find yourself having to deal with "NO." This is normal. With each "NO," you need to understand why not, and the step-by-step process needed to bring both parties closer together.

Negotiation checklist
- ☐ Do you understand the Customer-Centric situation?
    - ☐ What is the Impact our service is having on their business? (both emotional and rational)
    - ☐ What is the Critical Event Did you create a Critical Event Timeline?
    - ☐ What is the Decision criteria? Did you share this with the customer?

- ☐ Do you have all the key elements? (price, contract terms, payment terms)
- ☐ Is it closable today?   *If we come to an agreement can you commit to this by....*
- ☐ Is it with the right person?   *Am I right to assume you can make this decision*

Negotiation step-by-step

STEP 1 **Do you know the person on the other side of the table? Their way of responding etc.**

STEP 2 **Get all negotiation items on the table (i.e., price, terms, setup fee, etc.)**

STEP 3 **Repeat what you heard**   *So if I got it right you want ___ and ___*

STEP 4 **Ask,**   *Is there anything else?.*

STEP 5 **Prioritize the issues:**   *Let me ask, what is most important to you price or...*

Dig in, have a conversation, figure out what they really need.

STEP 6 **Summarize**   *So you want this and this.*

STEP 7 **Talking to decision maker?**   *If we come to an agreement today can you make the decision by {date}* **– If not ask what is holding them back.**

STEP 8 **Basics of negotiation:**
- Start with the easy ones.
- Give reluctantly and slowly.   *I'd like to work with you, here is what I can offer.*
- Keep track of all concessions and confirm in writing (email).
- Get something in return for every give.

STEP 9 Make the offer – do not hesitate, be clear and be concise

STEP 10 LISTEN and understand their counter-offer

STEP 11 Repeat the counter-offer — *Do I understand correctly that you would like...*

STEP 12 When you reach an agreement, repeat what you agreed on

STEP 13 If they ask for something new: — *That changes the deal.*

STEP 14 Add expiration date: — *Per our agreement, this deal expires on...*
Agree to consequences: — *If we miss that date the deal will reset to... fair enough?.*

STEP 16 Confirm immediately w/ email — *Per our conversation we agreed to... did I get that right?.*

STEP 17 Follow up with a contract — *As discussing in the email in which we agreed to...*

EXAMPLE Confirmation letter

Subject: Summary of the agreement

To: Denise, cc: Matt, Paul

Hi Denise –

This is a follow-up to our discussion regarding _____ project.

{{Your company name}} agrees to a price of $___/mo for an {{xx}} month contract. As part of this price concession, your company has agreed to the following:

- Purchase order to be received on or before February 27.

- A 12 month agreement with a monthly commit of $____, adjusted from $_____

The special pricing and terms of this agreement are to be held in the strictest confidence.

We also agree that the price becomes $____/mo if the contingency-free purchase order is not received on or before February 27.

Thank you for working with us. We are excited about the opportunity and greatly appreciate your business.

With kind regards,

Scott

BEST PRACTICES :

- **DO NOT** consider negotiation an event! It started long ago, and will not end.
- **DO** use the power word "fair," and the power sentence "that changes the deal."
- **DO NOT** negotiate by yourself.
- **DO** repeat back what the customer asks for "Do I understand that you are asking for…?"
- **DO NOT** be afraid of the NO; the NO tells you a lot more than a YES does.
- **DO** send a negotiation letter after the meeting to confirm the agreement.

PRO TIP Negotiation has changed over the past 2-3 years. Today you benefit from being very transparent in your approach, and making it crystal clear what you want to accomplish. This does not apply across all cultures around the world.

- JACCO VAN DER KOOIJ

7.3 Price Objections

Four major questions when confronted with *"Your price is too high"*

QUESTION 1 Ask, *"Compared with what?"* or *"Can you explain that?"* Asking your customer to elaborate to better understand the objection is essential to address that objection. *"I've received a lower bid from a competitor for the exact same offering as you."* If this is true, then you need to explain to your customer why your solution is worth more than the alternatives she is considering (go back to strategy, add services, etc).

QUESTION 2 *"Are you ready to commit now?"* Unless the customer is ready to buy now – not 4 months from now – there should be no pricing negotiations. Only if the customer is willing and able to commit, continue to question 3.

QUESTION 3 *"Is pricing the only remaining issue?"* Many times, customers "forget" to reveal to you that there are some major outstanding issues. They will tell you that the price is the only remaining issue, only to later unveil payment terms, delivery, warranty, or other key issues. This is handled with a powerful closing question: *"To confirm, you have no outstanding concerns on any other issues, correct?"*

QUESTION 4 *"Please share with me what the price difference is, and I'll do my very best to narrow the gap."* Your customer will typically respond with something like: *"I don't feel comfortable sharing that with you."* In that case, you do not have enough information to approach your manager and professionally request a lower price. You simply can't call your manager and say: "Our price is too high – I need a bigger discount." If your manager does give you a larger discount (doubtful) and you end up losing this opportunity, just imagine how poor you look in the eyes of your manager and company. At this point, you must get your customer to share where you need to be in order to earn the business. At a minimum, she should be willing to approximate the difference as a percentage range.

Once your customer provides you with their target price, you will then use a confirming summary close to insure that you have a full understanding of exactly where she stands and what you need to do to earn her business: *"So let me review: You indicated that you want to finalize your investment decision tomorrow, you are 110% convinced that we are the right solution for you and the only thing standing between us doing business is $X, correct?"*

This was contributed by Daniel J. Adams of Trust Triangle Selling. You can find his award-winning book on BUILDING TRUST, GROWING SALES on his web site: www.trusttriangleselling.com

7.4 Crazy Ivan

The "Crazy Ivan" is is a cold war term given to a maneuver used by Soviet submarines to clear their baffles to see if they were being followed. It achieved fame in the movie *The Hunt For Red October* with Sean Connery and Alec Baldwin. The maneuver involves the submarine randomly performing a 180 degree turn to catch an unsuspecting enemy trailing the submarine.

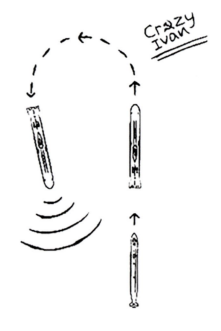

The Crazy Ivan in sales works very well when "The customer has verbally committed and we are just awaiting paperwork." Whilst you think that is the case, the customer is informing the other bidders on the project. Some of them will immediately engage their executives. These executive will start calling on the most senior person at the customer. Some will offer the 1st year of services for free. All the whilst you are dreaming of how to spend the commission.

In order to counter this you perform a CRAZY IVAN

STEP 1 **Call an emergency meeting because we lost the deal**

Announce that you've received a call that "we were down-selected." And call an immediate meeting, inviting key people/execs to the meeting!

STEP 2 **The setup**

In the meeting, announce that the deal was lost to XYZ based on ABC. Then ask the team to come-up with a plan and a list of activities for how we can recover from the loss. Look for activities that do not involve "discounting." We are looking for activities that can be implemented in the final weeks of the deal.

STEP 3 **The Deal**

Get the action plan pulled together, something like:

- Your exec fly to meet with their exec.
- Product team to make the missing feature available.
- The CS team to provide a detailed roll-out plan etc.

STEP 4 **The Crazy Ivan**

Announce to the team the "Crazy Ivan" – then as a team agree which actions should still take place.

7.5 Accelerated Close

How it works

All sales pros have quotas to fill by end of month/quarter deadlines. Sometimes you may need to accelerate a deal in order to meet your goals. And there are various tools that you can use to help accelerate deals to meet your goals. BUT – never ask the customer If they can "help you make your quota" or "get this in before the end of the quarter" – this is a big taboo and makes you look like a self-serving salesperson. Instead, find something that benefits them. You need to make them feel special!

Here is a great example of how you offer a customer a way to accelerate their decision.

STEP 1 **The intro**

Good morning Mike, how are you doing?

STEP 2 **The tease**

The reason I am calling you is that our VP of Sales approved special pricing that I can offer to the first 3 customers that sign by Thursday.

And considering our talks last week – I naturally thought of you.

STEP 3 **Present the offer with a timeframe creating exclusivity**

But before I make the offer, let me ask you ...

are you able to make a decision in this timeframe and execute paperwork?

IF YES...

STEP 4 **Make the offer (ONLY when they confirm they can commit)**

IF NO...

STEP 4 **Thank them – and confirm that the decision is still on for next month/quarter**

BEST PRACTICES

- **DO** use this on special occasions and with approval from your manager/VP of Sales.
- **DO** apply to deals that are at __%.
- **DO** practice 1-1 with your team beforehand – and proofread your email.

8 Commit

Congrats! You have helped your customer move to the next stage of finding a solution. They chose you to partner with, and now it's time to help transition them into becoming an onboarded customer. When you receive a verbal commit, the deal isn't done. There could easily still be a competitor in the running. This is the part where prices get dropped, and executives get involved, or worse – VCs or boards get involved. Thus, it is of utmost importance that you take the following actions:

CHECKLIST

- ☐ Deal processing. Expedite any paperwork: Set up immediate meetings with the purchasing team.
- ☐ Deal confirmation letter. Sent out a deal confirmation letter.
- ☐ Set up a debrief call. Secure the pros and cons of your solution.
- ☐ Send out a deal secure package, including some t-shirts and/or swag for the decision makers.
- ☐ Schedule the onboarding/training with a transfer call.
- ☐ Executive involvement: Get one of the execs to write a welcome note to the customer execs.
- ☐ ....
- ☐ ....
- ☐ ....
- ☐ ....

Confirm a win

When a customer has actually signed the contract, do the following:

- **DO** send a thank you note.
- **DO** .... (send swag or a welcome gift).
- **DO** .... (e.g., send a survey the experience).

Thank you and debrief

The moment a customer has committed to you and your company they have a vested interest to provide a lot more insight into the situation. This requires that you schedule a 1-1 debrief – a great way to schedule this is through the Thank You Note.

STEP 1 **Thank you note**

Aloke,

Thank you for choosing to go with [my company]. In an effort to help you <achieve goal> on set date I was hoping if we could briefly catch-up by phone later today? Is there a time convenient for you?

Best,

Nico

STEP 2 Call

- During the call:
    - Thank them for the business.
    - You can ask "What the trade-off was between your service and the others?"
- Inquire on the following:
    - What are the things you need to know to make this project a success?
    - How to make this project a success?
    - What help your customer needs from you to make this a success?

Asking for a referral
The request for referral is the easiest way, and after you have earned it, provides an incredible opportunity.

WHEN **Anytime! –** Asking for a referral can be done ANYTIME during the process. However, most people feel comfortable just after the close. Do not mistake that any positive interaction with a customer is a GREAT moment for asking for a referral.

WHO **Anyone! –** Not just CXOs and your SPONSOR can be asked for a referral. Anyone can.

WHAT **Two kinds**

- Asking a referral for yourself (LinkedIn Recommendation).
- Asking for intro into another deal (Anyone else interested?).

HOW **A few simple sentences:**

 Do you know of anyone else that can benefit from this solution?

If they provide you a referral ... **first and foremost** say this...

 THANK YOU!

They just provided you a referral ... that is extremely gracious of them! And Congratulations that is the ultimate compliment you get as a sales professional.

 Do you mind if I mention your name and that you encouraged me to reach out?

Obviously, having them introduce you is great. But often this can be forgotten etc. Instead, stay in control, reach out to the referral and cc: your referral. That way it will keep going!

NEXT **Thank you note and swag!**
- Send a handwritten postcard to thank them.
- If you have access to company swag, send it to them to thank them.

9 Not a fit

9.1 Debrief with the Customer

When a customer informs you that their decision is "no', what should you do?

- **STEP 1** Schedule a 5-minute debrief.
- **STEP 2** Send a thank you note.
- **STEP 3** Update your records processes – e.g. does the customer still wish to receive your product updates.
- **STEP 4** Execute exit process (NDA, Logo removal, Use-case removal etc.).

When they inform you of the loss – reply expressing gratitude for getting back to you, and for the opportunity. Ask if you can have 5 minutes of their time to get their feedback. Customers are likely going to give you information that is not necessarily correct, and this can lead to you setting your company up for failure. For example, they can say the price was too high – and now you are dropping price across the entire business?

NO! Instead simply focus the entire call on; "What was the trade-off that you made?"

BEST PRACTICES

- **DO** focus on obtaining the key points where your competitor was strong and weak; try to identify why your strong points were not valued over the competitor's weak points.
- **DO NOT** battle the customer.
- **DO NOT** state "oh but we do that too" even If they completely missed your value prop – it will not work at this time. Rather take the info back, revise the offer and come back within an hour!

- **DO** take solid notes, and record the call.
- **DO** prepare questions and listen carefully.
- **DO** agree with the customer on the next steps, even if there are none – but perhaps – check in 30 days from now. Most likely your competitor is going to mess up the onboarding, or the CEO may resign, the AE might botch the deal, etc. You never know!
- **DO** find out the length of the contract they are signing – so you can set a reminder to approach them again a few months before it's time to renew.

9.2 Confirm the Loss

You've made it this far in the playbook, so you know how valuable your personal brand is. You've invested a ton of time in helping to educate the customer, guiding them through the process and leveraging best practices. Then the worst happens – they say no.

Stay in it for the long haul. You never know if the other solution they went with was oversold.

The best way to stand out: Write a handwritten card. This will make you stand head and shoulders above the competition. The objective of the loss note is to leave a very memorable professional impression.

Ryan,

Thank you for spending time with me over the past few weeks. I thoroughly enjoyed the interaction with you. Although I am naturally disappointed that we won't be working together, I do look forward to staying in touch. I will occasionally check back in to make sure you are doing well. Either way, here is my phone number: _____ and email address in case anything comes up.

Best,

Michelle

Summary

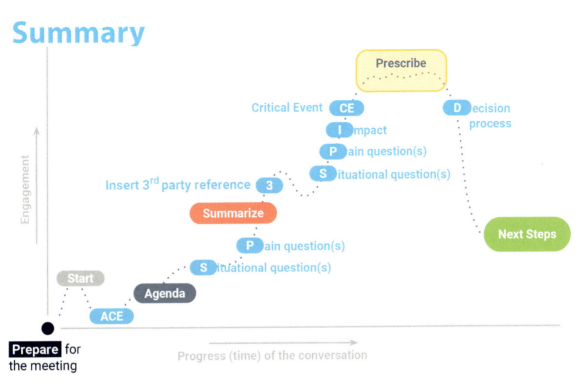

	Outline Of A Discovery Call	**Prepare**
ACE Opening	• **A**ppreciate you taking the time. • **C**onfirm end time, are we still good till ... • **E**nd goal of this call, we agree to...	*Determine what you want the outcome of the meeting to be!*
Agenda	• Confirm the agenda you sent in calendar invite. • Ask customer for their goals. • Make sure you involve everyone. • Summarize goals, ask "is there anything else?" • Set priorities to hit end time.	*Research everyone on the meeting (2-3 mins/ person)*

	Outline Of A Discovery Call	**Prepare**
SPI Diagnose	• Ask **S**ituational questions • Identify **P**ain • **Summarize S S P** • **Ask** "Did I get that right?" • **Empathize** "I hear this a lot." • **Mention** a **3**rd-party relevant to pain.	*Prepare a list of questions, and structure them into . . including reference case-studies*
Prescribe	Make a recommendation following what "others in the same situation" have done. Be specific what happened. • **Why** – Sharing your market insights. • **How** – The approach, how would it look & feel? • **What** – What we are specifics we do. • **Proof** – Benefits customers have experienced.	*Know use-case stories relevant to the customer*
ICED Qualify	• **I**mpact on the business (**$$$**, **cost**, **UX/UI**) • **C**ritical **E**vent "what happens if ... miss." • **D**ecision Criteria/Process	*Prepare a list of critical events that may apply.*

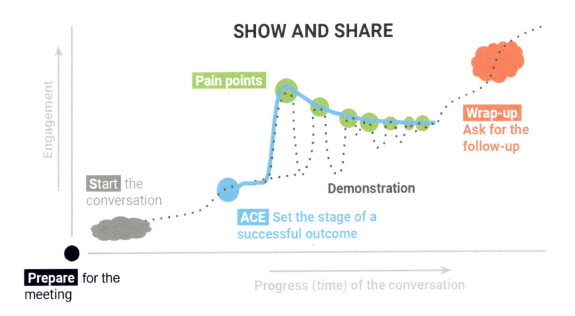

Show & Share	Outline Of A Demonstration	Prepare
Demonstration	• Set the stage with what you will demo. • Address each pain point one at a time. **Per Pain-Point** • Orient them/Describe the screen • Demo / Share use-cases • Ask "Can you see … using the service" • Ask "What impact … would it have" • LISTEN and follow the conversation **SUMMARIZE** if the points were addressed/ anything else.	*Have a script to their pain points.* *Set Up your tabs in a browser.*

Wrap-Up	**ACE** You earned the right to ask for the business – refer to the "E" – End Goal of the meeting.	
	First "Did we address your questions to your satisfaction?"	*What to ask for!*
	Then "At the beginning of the call we said… "	
	Ask "May I ask are you ready to… {{move forward}} "	

Selection	Outline of Decision Criteria	
Assist Selection	**Step 1** Determine Decision Criteria	
	Step 2 Prioritize	
	Step 3 Determine options	
	Step 4 Determine our position	
Assist Buying	Reprioritize (up/down)	
	Insert new criteria	
	Improve ranking (involve a new DM)	

OPTIONS: You, Competitor, No action

DECISION CRITERIA	You	Competitor	No action
1. Performance	1	2	3
2. NEW Criteria	1	2	3
3. Feature X	3	2	1
4. Price	2	3	1

Conclusion

At the beginning of this book we laid out the various selling methodologies a SaaS company can pursue to grow revenue. From DIY Self Service to Provocative Selling, each approach has pros and cons and requires a solid understanding of your company's Product, GTM, and market position in order to implement correctly. Each methodology also has a set of activities that best suit its specifics and variations in how you should message your offer. Not only that, but the channels you use for each will differ.

Hopefully, however, you learned more than just some selling methodologies. The more important lesson we would like you to come away with is that your customer views their experience very differently from you. So, when you choose to engage in something like Provocative Selling, the reason for doing so should always be that your target customers do not even know they have a problem yet. And you should modify your messaging and process to match.

Last, you may or may not have noticed, but in this book we stayed away from the term "closing" and generally avoided the hunting metaphors that often come with selling. That is because the world has changed, and "the sale" is no longer really "the sale." It's just a temporary commitment while your customer tries your product. We do hope, however, that with the detailed processes and methodologies in this book you will be much more effective at helping your customers commit.

Abbreviations Used in this Book

People:
  AE: Account Executive
  AM: Account Manager
  BDR: Business Development Representative
  CSM: Customer Success Manager
  CEO: Chief Executive Officer
  CRO: Chief Revenue Officer
  CCO: Chief Customer Officer
  FAE: Field Account Executive
  MDR: Marketing Development Representative
  PM: Product Manager
  SDR: Sales Development Representative
  SE: Sales Engineer, sometimes refers to a web developer
  VPM: VP Marketing
  VPS: VP Sales

SaaS Lead Definition:
  Suspect: A person who may be interested
  Prospect: A person who expresses interest
  MQL: Marketing Qualified Lead, a person who expresses interest and fits the profile.
  SQL: Sales Qualified Lead, person who is interested
  SAL: Sales Accepted Lead
  WIN: A client who commits to the service
  LIVE: Client who has been onboarded

SaaS Business:
  ACV: Annual Contract Value
  ACRC: Annual Customer Retention Cost
  ARR: Annual Recurring Revenue equal to 12 times MRR
  B2B: Business to Business
  B4B: Business for Business
  B2C: Business to Consumer

CAC: Client Acquisition Cost, the amount to acquire a single client
CR: Conversion Ratio, the amount of leads to produce one SQL
CRC: Client Retention Cost, the cost to retain a client for 12 months
CRM: Customer Relationship Management (platform)
CSM: Customer Success Management (platform)
ENT: Enterprises, companies with over 5,000 employees
LOGO: Common use term for a high-value client
LTV: Lifetime Value of a client, often between 3-5 times ACV
MAS: Marketing Automation Software (platform)
MRR: Monthly Recurring Revenue
PTC: Refers to the combined cost of (P)eople, (T)ools, and (C)ontent
RoI: Return on Investment
SaaS: Software as a Service
SC: Sales Cycle
SMB: Small to Medium Business(es) often between 50-500 employees
SME: Small to Medium Enterprise often between 500-5k employees
VSB: Very Small Business often between 2-50 employees
PRO: Prosumer, a single user who behaves like a business user
WR: Win Ratio, the number of accounts it takes to produce one WIN In the years since we published "Blueprints," we have been amazed at the response we have gotten from sales professionals in multiple fields, not just SaaS. It has been humbling!

About Winning By Design

Winning By Design was founded by Jacco Van Der Kooij with the purpose of helping SaaS companies level up their sales game in the face of radically compressed sales cycles and lower price points. We teach fundamental sales skills and combine them with process and systems to create self-teaching sales organizations.

To find out more about our offerings please visit:
www.saassalesmethod.com

Made in the USA
Coppell, TX
13 April 2022